THE THIRD REICH FROM ORIGINAL SOURCES

THIRD REICH PROPAGANDA

BOB CARRUTHERS

Pen & Sword
MILITARY

This edition published in 2013 by
Pen & Sword Military
An imprint of
Pen & Sword Books Ltd
47 Church Street
Barnsley
South Yorkshire
S70 2AS

First published in Great Britain in 2012 in digital format by
Coda Books Ltd.

Copyright © Coda Books Ltd, 2012
Published under licence by Pen & Sword Books Ltd.

ISBN 978 1 78159 210 6

The right of Bob Carruthers to be identified as Author of this work has been asserted by him in
accordance with the Copyright, Designs and Patents Act 1988.

A CIP catalogue record for this book is
available from the British Library.

Printed and bound by CPI Group (UK) Ltd, Croydon, CR0 4YY

Pen & Sword Books Ltd incorporates the Imprints of Pen & Sword Aviation, Pen & Sword
Family History, Pen & Sword Maritime, Pen & Sword Military, Pen & Sword Discovery, Pen
& Sword Politics, Pen & Sword Atlas, Pen & Sword Archaeology, Wharncliffe Local History,
Wharncliffe True Crime, Wharncliffe Transport, Pen & Sword Select, Pen & Sword Military
Classics, Leo Cooper, The Praetorian Press, Claymore Press, Remember When, Seaforth
Publishing and Frontline Publishing

For a complete list of Pen & Sword titles please contact
PEN & SWORD BOOKS LIMITED
47 Church Street, Barnsley, South Yorkshire, S70 2AS, England
E-mail: enquiries@pen-and-sword.co.uk
Website: www.pen-and-sword.co.uk

CONTENTS

THE VÖLKISCHER BEOBACHTER

I N DECEMBER 1920 with the help of Dietrich Eckhart and
a personal loan, which Anton Drexler subscribed for, the
fledgling National Socialist party scraped together the finance
to acquire the *Völkischer Beobachter*. This right wing newspaper,
owned by as *Völkischer Beobachter* was destined to become the
main organ of the Nazi party. The paper had formerly been known
as the *Münchner Beobachter* and it was known by this title when
it was acquired by the Thule Society in 1918. In August 1919 was
renamed *Völkischer Beobachter*.

The NSDAP purchase of the paper in December 1920 was
largely on the initiative of Dietrich Eckart, who became the first
editor. Later, in 1921, Adolf Hitler acquired all shares in the
company, making him the sole owner of the publication. It is
interesting to note the juxtaposition of name of the publication
with Hitler's political creed. In 1920 Hitler's immediate concern
was to distance the party from esoteric aspects of the *völkisch*
movement which were growing in influence and had adopted a
range of increasingly bizarre ideas dredged up from Germany's
mythology and relied upon revived 'folk memories' of her ancient
past. As well as their strange behaviour Hitler also despised the
timidity of the *völkisch* leaders who were content to hide behind
quasi-masonic secret societies. He claims he did not set much
store on the friendship of people who did not succeed in getting
disliked by their enemies. Therefore, he considered the friendship
of such people as not only worthless but even dangerous to his
young movement:

*"That was the principal reason why we first called ourselves
a party. We hoped that by giving ourselves such a name we might
scare away a whole host of völkisch dreamers. And that was
the reason also why we named our Party, the National Socialist*

German Workers Party. It was not without good reason that when we laid down a clearly defined programme for the new movement we excluded the word völkisch from it. The concept underlying the term völkisch cannot serve as the basis of a movement, because it is too indefinite and general in its application."

Not content with his lengthy exposition, Hitler kept on railing at great length against the *völkisch* influences. On page after page of *Mein Kampf* he vents his spleen against the *völkisch* fringe. Hitler clearly had a major issue with those who went around beating the big drum for the *völkisch* idea. His long and incoherent rant against the *völkisch* movement demonstrates that by 1924 the whole concept had clearly become a major irritant to Hitler. There can be little doubt that his rant is aimed at Lanz von Leibenfels and his ilk. The followers of the Esoteric Germanic mystics had formed mystical orders including the New Templars. According to Hitler the full name of the new party kept away the champions of the *völkisch* movement:

"… those heroes whose weapon is the sword of the spirit and all those whining poltroons who take refuge behind their so-called 'intelligence' as if it were a kind of shield."

Despite his hatred of what the *völkisch* movement had by then become, Hitler did nothing to change the name of the paper. We must assume that while he went to some lengths to exclude the word *völkisch* from his party he was always content to have it associated with his newspaper. This was typical of the type of contradiction which Hitler created throughout his life, he often sought to have more than one horse running in a race and, notwithstanding his seemingly unbridled prejudice, he was content to allow the title of this key publication to remain unchanged, it would appear he was only too aware of the power of the *völkisch* ideas at the ballot box and was happy to benefit from that by association.

Initially the paper appeared twice weekly; but at the beginning of 1923 it became a daily paper, and at the end of August in the same year it began to appear in the large broadsheet format giving the paper an up-market veneer which was certainly not justified by the tone of its contents. For twenty-five years the *Völkischer Beobachter* formed a key part of the official public face of the Nazi party. The paper quickly became dubbed as the "fighting paper of the National Socialist movement of Greater Germany" (*Kampfblatt der nationalsozialistischen Bewegung Grossdeutschlands*).

In 1921, Hitler immersed himself in the running of the paper, but as a complete novice in publishing, he soon learned many commercial lessons for which, by his own admission, he had to pay dearly. By Hitler's paranoid reasoning the number of papers in Jewish hands, meant there was at that time only one important newspaper that defended the cause of the German people. For Hitler this was a matter for grave concern and the *Völkischer Beobachter* was the only a popular organ which championed his views.

Hitler soon discovered that the new acquisition had all the correct journalistic qualities, but it was soon clear that Freiher von

A 1920 poster designed by Adolf Hitler at the time when he was the head of propaganda. This poster lacks the visual impact of later campaigns. This was probably a result of the chronic lack of funding.

Sebottendorf hadn't sold the paper for purely altruistic reasons. Commercially, the paper was a disaster just waiting to happen. Hitler soon recognised that he was out of his depth and conceded its management as a business concern was simply impossible. Hitler, for once, recognised that the scale of the problem was beyond his limited experience and sought to alter matters as promptly as he could. Financial disaster loomed and Lucky Linzer now needed some of his trademark good luck, and as frequently happened, luck was on his side. It appeared in the shape of a chance meeting with a former Great War colleague. In 1914, in the trenches of the Great War, Hitler recollected how he had made the acquaintance of Max Amann, who was then his superior. Amann had a great deal of entrepreneurial flair and would later become the general business Director of the Party. During four years in the War, Hitler had abundant opportunities to observe what he later described as the unusual ability, diligence and the rigorous conscientiousness of his future collaborator:

"In the summer of 1921, I applied to my old regimental comrade, whom I met one day by chance, and asked him to become business manager of the movement. At that time the movement was passing through a grave crisis and I had reason to be dissatisfied with several of our officials, with one of whom I had had a very bitter experience. Amann then held a good situation in which there were also good prospects for him. After long hesitation he agreed to my request, but only on condition that he must not be at the mercy of incompetent committees. He must be responsible to one master, and only one. It is to the inestimable credit of this first business manager of the party, whose commercial knowledge is extensive and profound, that he brought order and probity into the various offices of the party. Since that time these have remained exemplary and cannot be equalled or excelled in this by any other branches of the movement. But, as often happens in life, great ability provokes envy and disfavour. That had also to be expected in this case and borne patiently."

Without the entrepreneurial skills of Amann to call upon, the acquisition of the *Völkischer Beobachter* could well have resulted in financial meltdown which would have signified the end of the NSDAP, but ownership of the paper was essential to everything that Hitler envisaged and was especially important for a number of well thought out reasons. When he entered the DAP, as it was then known, Hitler at once took charge of the propaganda function. From his experience in the Great War, he correctly believed the most important political activity was the control and influence of the press. He understood the power of the press and had railed against it at length during the Great War. His overriding objective was to spread the new ideas among as many people as possible, as fast as possible, and a tame newspaper was one obvious way to achieve that end.

Propaganda was to become synonymous with the National Socialist movement, but it is the bedrock on which every political

(Left) From the outset the swastika (or Hagekreuz as it was known) provided the Nazi party with a powerful and distinctive graphic symbol. The word swastika was unknown in Nazi circles within Germany. (Right) A powerful electoral image focuses Nazi opposition against the Dawes plan.

party and regimes and institutions of every political hue are founded. The terrible crimes of the Nazi regime understandably overshadow the fact that Hitler was first and foremost a formidable politician, his fearsome oratorical skills made him a communicator par excellence and his self study programme in art and design contributed to his powerful record as propagandist, the like of which the world had not yet witnessed. Long before Goëbbels came on the scene, Hitler had formed a highly credible and practical understanding of the mechanics of mass communication and advertising and he instinctively understood how eye catching graphic design could be effectively harnessed to shape public opinion. It is an uncomfortable truth, but many of the tactics practised by today's politicians which are now so commonplace, were developed and road tested by Adolf Hitler.

As director of propaganda for the party, Hitler took care to shape the output of the *Völkischer Beobachter* very carefully. Under the editorship of the talented Deitrich Eckhart, the lively and combative style of the paper was neatly dovetailed to conform to the cohesive style and form which Hitler gave to all the early propaganda. Hitler was therefore able to claim with some satisfaction that it was due to the effect of his propaganda that within a short period of time hundreds of thousands of citizens became convinced in their hearts that the policies of the NSDAP were somehow right for Germany.

THE BIRTH OF THE SWASTIKA

Hitler's innate understanding of the power of imagery soon led him to the conclusion that the major disadvantage for the party lay in the fact that members of the party possessed no unifying outward symbol of membership which linked them together. Hitler soon set to work on the problem and immediately recalled from his youth the psychological impact of the red-black-gold symbols of 1848 were to the *Deututscher Schulverein* (German

Schools Association) to which Hitler had once belonged. His understanding of the power of a political symbol arose not just from a sentimental point of view. In Berlin, after the War, Hitler was present at a mass-demonstration of Marxists in front of the Royal Palace and in the *Lustgarten*. He described how the sea of red flags, red armlets and red flowers was sufficient to give that huge assembly of about 120,000 people an outward appearance of strength. Hitler recorded that by 1920 he was able to feel and understand how easily the man in the street succumbs to the hypnotic magic of such a grandiose piece of theatrical presentation.

The problem for Hitler was that his party inclined towards the right, the natural province of the bourgeoisie, which as a group neither possessed nor stood for any easily digestible *weltanschauung*. Hitler refers to this group "The bourgeoisie" as the natural pool of supporters for the nationalist cause. A better translation might be obtained by the substitution of the word conservative for "bourgeoisie" as Hitler was referring to their outlook on the world rather than their economic status. He noted that the conservatives had no rallying banner and simply sported the black-white-red colours of the second German Reich and eschewed the new German Reich the Black-Red-Gold design which was chosen as the flag of the German Republic founded at Weimar in 1919. Hitler reasoned that this new Reich was morticed together without the aid of the conservatives and the flag itself was born of the post war events and was therefore merely a State flag possessing no importance in the sense of any particular ideological mission.

Hitler noted that up until 1920, in opposition to the Marxists, there was no flag that would have represented a rallying point for a consolidated resistance to them. For even if the political elements of the German bourgeoisie were loath to accept the suddenly discovered black, red and gold colours as their symbol, after the year 1918, they nevertheless were incapable of counteracting this with a future programme of their own.

To Hitler's way of thinking the conservatives were likely to warm to a return to the values of the Second Reich, hence the resurrection of the black, white and red colours of the old German war flag. It was obvious to Hitler however, that the symbol of a régime which had been overthrown by the Marxists under inglorious circumstances, was not now worthy to serve as a banner under which Marxism was to be crushed. He assumed that however much many Germans may have loved and revered those old colours, that flag was now tainted by failure and Hitler appreciated that it had little value for the struggle of the future.

Hitler adopted the standpoint that it was actually a lucky development for the German nation that it had lost its old flag, the National Socialists recognised that hoisting the old colours would not symbolise their new aims:

"for we had no wish to resurrect from the dead the old Reich which had been ruined through its own blunders, but to build up a new state."

(Left) 'The Last Grenade' depicts a great war soldier in the trenches. It was one of Hitler's favourite paintings and was widely re-worked during World War II. (Right) This development on the theme of the last grenade is an impressive example of Third Reich war art.

Hitler subscribed to the view that the new movement which was fighting Marxism along these new lines must display on its banner the symbol of the new State. The question of the new flag was an important issue and one which could not easily be resolved. Suggestions poured in from all quarters, but Hitler would not be rushed as he knew that a really striking emblem might be the first stimulus which could cause an awakening interest in his movement.

For this reason Hitler declined all suggestions from various quarters for identifying the movement by means of a predominantly white flag like that of the old state. He reasoned that white is not a colour capable of attracting and focusing public attention. For him it was a colour suitable only for "young women's associations" and not at all appropriate for a movement that stands for reform in a revolutionary period. Hitler tells us that black was also suggested and he considered it certainly well-suited to the times, but embodying no significance to empress the will behind the national Socialist movement and again incapable of attracting attention.

White and blue was discarded, despite what Hitler called its admirable aesthetic appeal, as being the colours, depending on the hue, of either Bavaria or Prussia, and generally speaking, with these colours it would have been difficult to attract attention to the movement. The same applied to black and white. Hitler also recalled that black, red and gold did not enter the question at all as they were associated with the Weimar Republic.

Hitler finally settled on a combination of black, white and red as, in his view, the effectiveness of these three colours was far superior to all the others and formed, in his opinion, the most strikingly harmonious combination to be found. Hitler was always for keeping the old black-white–red colours, because as a soldier he regarded them as his most sacred possession and also he claimed that in their aesthetic effect, they conformed more than anything else to his personal taste. Accordingly he claimed he had to discard all the innumerable suggestions and designs which had been proposed for the new movement, among which were many that had incorporated the swastika into the old colours. Hitler claimed that, as leader of the party, he was unwilling to make public his own self created and highly favoured design, on the grounds that it was possible that someone else could come forward with a design just as good, if not better, than his own. Somewhat predictably Hitler eventually decided that his own design was the best all along and the time had come to reveal his masterpiece to a waiting world:

"After innumerable trials I decided upon a final form, a flag of red material with a white disc bearing in its centre a black swastika. After many trials I obtained the correct proportions between the dimensions of the flag and of the white central disc, as well as that of the swastika. And this is how it has remained ever since."

(Left) A stock NSDAP poster which could be customised to advertise a local event. (Right) An early Nazi election poster urges the veterans among the electorate to rally behind Hitler as a former comrade who truly understands the sacrifice made by 2,000,000 German soldiers.

Hitler is likely to have encountered and imbibed various *völkisch* concepts, touching on Germanic mythology and mysticism from his time at Lambach choir school onwards. It was certainly the case that the former abbot Father Hagn had ordered the Hakenkreuz (swastika shaped) designs carved on the Lambach abbey entrance way as early as 1868. Although this is likely to have been a harmless pun on his name and it is highly likely that this would have been Hitler's first encounter with the symbol which widely adopted *völkisch* movement. It should be noted that Hitler did not at any time refer to this design as a "swastika", to him it was always a Hakenkreuz or hooked cross. The word 'swastika' was put into Hitler's mouth by translators of *Mein Kampf*, beginning with James Murphy.

The new flag appeared in public in the midsummer of 1920. It suited the new movement admirably, both being new and innovative. Not a soul had seen this flag before it's unveiling and Hitler recorded that its effect at that time was something akin to that of a blazing torch. Hitler recalled how he experienced an almost a boyish delight when one of the ladies of the party who had been entrusted with the making of the flag finally handed it over for the first time. A few months later the party in Munich was in possession of six of these flags.

Hitler was ecstatic over his latest creation, not only because it incorporated what he termed "those revered colours" expressive of a homage to what Hitler called the "glorious past". The key to the design obviously lay in the visually arresting Swastika design. For Hitler, this *völkisch* symbol was also an eloquent visual expression of the will behind the movement. For a modern readership it has become synonymous with evil on such an unimaginable scale that it is almost impossible to approach this icon of the twentieth century with any measure of objectivity as a piece of graphic design. We have to be satisfied with the fact that, by any objective measure, the new symbol satisfied all the criteria which surrounded its creation. It was eye catching, interesting and dynamic and from the outset, Hitler was prone to boasting over the qualities of what is now universally recognised as a symbol of unbridled malevolence:

"We National Socialists regarded our flag as being the embodiment of our party programme. The red expressed the social thought underlying the movement. White the national thought. And the swastika signified the mission allotted to us--the struggle for the victory of Aryan mankind and at the same time the triumph of the ideal of creative work which is in itself and always will be anti-Semitic."

As soon as the new symbol was unveiled, Hitler immediately ordered the corresponding armlets for the small squad of men who kept order at meetings. The steadily increasing strength of the hall guards over the next few months and years was a main factor in popularizing the new symbol. Two years later, when the small squads of hall guards had grown into the feared *Sturm Abteilung* (SA) (Storm Detachments), Hitler deemed it necessary to give this aggressive organization of young a particular standard of its own. He therefore designed a neo-classical banner topped with gold which harked back to the Roman legions. Hitler entrusted the execution of this new piece of political paraphernalia to an old party comrade, Herr Gahr, who was a goldsmith. This peculiar standard became the distinctive token of the SA and it was to become featured in huge numbers as National Socialist party mushroomed spreading fear throughout Germany.

- C H A P T E R 2 -
ENTER STREICHER

I T WAS at this unfortunate juncture that Hitler met the man who, with the exception of Dietrich Eckhart, would do more to shape his views than any other individual. Julius Striecher was a bullheaded political rough house and rabble rouser from Nuremberg. He was a fanatical anti-semite who would go on to publish '*Der Stürmer*', the notorious anti-semitical journal which would later form Hitler's favourite reading. The meeting between Hitler and Streicher is often overlooked and it provides a very plausible explanation for the problem which has vexed historians. During his Vienna period, Hitler undoubtedly held strongly anti-semitic views in the mould of Schönerer or Wolf. The reasons are less clear why Hitler developed from a mainstream anti-semite to a full blown dyed-in-the-wool vicious ultra anti-semite capable of sanctioning mass murder on an unimaginable scale. In 1920 Hitler had fallen under the influence of Eckart who was a fierce anti-semite. Eckart was Hitler's mentor and it is certain that he wielded a great deal of influence. The entrance of Julius Streicher brought a rougher edge and may hold the final clue to the final transformation from Hitler as a committed opponent of Jewry into fully fledged anti-semite and arch enemy of the Jews.

Striecher prided himself on his self-imposed reputation as 'The number one Jew baiter "and as such his legacy is viewed with disdain. His career and the faux pornographic rantings of his publications are so odious that many serious historians are understandably reluctant to immerse themselves in the Streicher mire. As a result Streicher is marginalized and relegated to the status of a fringe character. This was not the case from Hitler's perspective. Streicher had a major influence on Hitler and he is one of the few Nazi era figures to be accorded a glowing personal testimonial in the pages of *Mein Kampf*. Hitler was grateful to Striecher for his willingness to submit to Hitler's growing influence and merge into the NSDAP a significant proportion of the *Deutsche Werkgemeinschaft*, a Nuremberg based nationalist umberella movement, complete with it's own newspaper, the *Deutscher Volkswille*. This unexpected development gave Hitler a foothold outside of Munich and provided a taste of similar successes to come. It was not to prove a smooth transition as Nuremberg would soon become the scene of tedious infighting between Streicher and his great rival Walther Kellerbauer, but the merger provided the first rung on the bridge to the north and began the process of expanding the party beyond its Munich roots. From that point onwards Streicher was a frequent and welcome visitor in Munich and he played a prominent role in the growth of the NSDAP. By virtue of his prominent position Streicher also had a large part to play in the concomitant entrenchment of anti-semitic policies. By 1921 Hitler was surrounded by virulent anti-semites

(Left) Germany Awake! This simple message was one of the early rallying calls for the Nazi party. (Right) 'Workers awake!' forms a powerful call to action in this election poster.

who could deliver their message in high flown tones of Eckart or in the vicious language of the gutter dwelling Streicher. The result was that the anti-Semitic aspects of party policy became increasingly prominent and ultimately took on the same importance as the nationalist elements as it became ingrained at the centre of the party's agenda.

Streicher was born in Fleinhausen, Kingdom of Bavaria, one of nine children of the teacher Friedrich Streicher and his wife Anna (née Weiss). He worked as an elementary school teacher like his father, and in 1909 he began his political career, joining the German Democratic Party. He would later claim that because his political work brought him into contact with German Jews, he "must therefore have been fated to become later on a writer and speaker on racial politics." In 1913 Streicher married Kunigunde Roth, a baker's daughter, in Nuremberg. They had two sons, Lothar (born 1915) and Elmar (born 1918).

Streicher joined the German Army in 1914. He won the Iron Cross and reached the rank of lieutenant by the time the Armistice was signed in November, 1918.

In 1919 Streicher became active in the anti-Semitic *Deutschvölkischer Schutz und Trutzbund* (German Nationalist Protection and Defense Federation), one of the various radical-nationalist organizations that sprang up in the wake of the failed German Communist revolution of 1918. Such groups fostered the view that Jews had conspired with "Bolshevik" traitors in trying to subject Germany to Communist rule. In 1920 he turned to the *Deutschsozialistische Partei* (German-Socialist Party), a group whose platform was close to that of the young NSDAP, or *National Sozialistische Deutsche Arbeiter Partei* (National Socialist German Worker's Party). Streicher sought to move the German-Socialists in a more virulently anti-Semitic direction – an effort which aroused enough opposition that he left the group and brought his now-substantial following to yet another organization in 1921, the *Deutsche Werkgemeinschaft* (German Working

Community), which hoped to unite the various anti-Semitic *Völkisch* movements.

In 1921, Streicher finally found his mentor. He visited Munich in order to hear Adolf Hitler speak, an experience that he later said left him transformed:

"I had never seen the man before. And there I sat, an unknown among unknowns. I saw this man shortly before midnight, after he had spoken for three hours, drenched in perspiration, radiant. My neighbour said he thought he saw a halo around his head, and I experienced something which transcended the commonplace."

Soon after, Streicher joined the Nazi Party and merged his personal following with Hitler's, almost doubling the party membership.

In May 1923 Streicher founded the newspaper, *Der Stürmer* (The Stormer). From the outset, the chief aim of the paper was to promulgate anti-Semitic propaganda. "We will be slaves of the Jew," the paper announced. "Therefore he must go."

(Left) The catholic church and the red menace are the enemies in this Munich election poster calling on the voters to choose list two.
(Right) For work and bread vote Hitler list two.

In November of that year, Streicher participated in Hitler's first effort to seize power, the failed Beer Hall Putsch in Munich. Streicher marched with Hitler in the front row of the would-be revolutionaries and braved the bullets of the Munich police. His loyalty earned him Hitler's lifelong trust and protection; in the years that followed, Streicher would be one of the dictator's few true intimates.

As a reward for his dedication, when the Nazi Party was legalized again and re-organized in 1925 Streicher was appointed *Gauleiter* of the Bavarian region of Franconia (which included his home town of Nuremberg). In the early years of the party's rise, *Gauleiter* were essentially party functionaries without real power; but in the final years of the Weimar Republic, they became paramilitary commanders. During the 12 years of the Nazi regime itself, party *Gauleiter* like Streicher would wield immense power, and be in large measure untouchable by legal authority.

Streicher was also elected to the Bavarian "Landtag" or legislature, a position which gave him a margin of parliamentary immunity - a safety net that would help him resist efforts to silence his racist message.

Beginning in 1924, Streicher used *Der Stürmer* as a mouthpiece not only for general anti-semitic attacks, but for calculated smear campaigns against specific Jews, such as the Nuremberg city official Julius Fleischmann, who worked for Streicher's nemesis, mayor Hermann Luppe. *Der Stürmer* accused Fleischmann of stealing socks from his quartermaster during combat in World War I. Fleischmann sued Streicher and successfully disproved the allegations in court (Streicher was fined 900 marks), but the detailed testimony exposed other less-than-glorious details of Fleischmann's record, and his reputation was badly damaged anyway. It was proof that Streicher's unofficial motto for his tactics was correct: "Something always sticks."

The slanderous attacks continued, and lawsuits followed. Like Fleischmann, other outraged German Jews defeated Streicher in court, but his goal was not necessarily legal victory; he wanted the widest possible dissemination of his message, which press coverage often provided. The rules of the court provided Streicher with an arena to humiliate his opponents, and he characterized the inevitable courtroom loss as a badge of honour. The Weimar habit of following the strictest letter of the law made prosecution for more serious crimes difficult. *Der Stürmer's* infamous official slogan, *Die Juden sind unser Unglück* (the Jews are our misfortune) was deemed unactionable under German statutes, since it was not a direct incitement to violence. During the thirties the phrase was adopted by the NSDAP and was widely used at rallies and speeches.

Streicher's opponents complained to authorities that *Der Stürmer* violated a statute against religious offense with his constant promulgation of the "blood libel" - the medieval accusation that Jews killed Christian children to use their blood to make matzoh. Streicher argued that his accusations were based on race, not religion, and that his communications were political speech, and therefore protected by the German constitution.

(Left) A 1931 election poster. (Right) A 1932 poster advertising a speech by Julius Streicher on the familiar theme, 'The Jews are our misfortune.'

Streicher orchestrated his early campaigns against Jews to make the most extreme possible claims, short of violating a law that might get the paper shut down. He insisted in the pages of his newspaper that the Jews had caused the worldwide Depression, and were responsible for the crippling unemployment and inflation which afflicted Germany during the 1920s. He claimed that Jews were white-slavers and were responsible for over 90 percent of the prostitutes in the country. Real unsolved killings in Germany, especially of children or women, were often confidently explained in the pages of *Der Stürmer* as cases of "Jewish ritual murder."

One of Streicher's constant themes was the sexual violation of ethnically German women by Jews, a subject which served as an excuse to publish semi-pornographic tracts and images detailing degrading sexual acts. These "essays" proved an especially appealing feature of the paper for young men. With the help of his notorious cartoonist, Phillip "Fips" Rupprecht, Streicher published image after image of Jewish stereotypes and sexually-charged encounters. His portrayal of Jews as subhuman and evil is widely considered to have played a critical role in the dehumanization and marginalization of the Jewish minority in the eyes of common Germans - creating the necessary conditions for the later perpetration of the Holocaust.

Streicher also combed the pages of the Talmud and the Old Testament in search of passages which could paint their ancient Jewish authors as harsh or cruel, a practice which continues to this day among anti-Semites. In 1929, this close study of Jewish scripture helped convict Streicher in a case known as "The Great Nuremberg Ritual Murder Trial." His familiarity with Jewish text was proof to the court that his attacks were religious in nature; Streicher was found guilty and imprisoned for two months. In Germany, press reaction to the trial was highly critical of Streicher; but the *Gauleiter* was greeted after his conviction by hundreds of cheering supporters, and within months Nazi party membership surged to its highest levels yet.

In April 1933, after Nazi control of the German state apparatus gave the *Gauleiters* enormous power, Streicher organised a one-day boycott of Jewish businesses which was used as a dress-rehearsal for other anti-Semitic commercial measures. As he consolidated his hold on power, he came to more or less rule the city of Nuremberg and his *Gau Franken*. Among the nicknames provided by his enemies were "King of Nuremberg" and the "Beast of Franconia." Because of his role as *Gauleiter* of Franconia, he also gained the nickname of *Frankenführer*.

To protect himself from accountability, Streicher relied on Hitler's protection. Hitler declared that *Der Stürmer* was his favourite newspaper, and saw to it that each weekly issue was posted for public reading in special glassed-in display cases known as "*Stürmerkasten*". The newspaper reached a peak circulation of 600,000 in 1935.

A powerful depiction of a Nazi torch-lit parade has all the hallmarks of Goebbels highly effective Ministry of Propaganda.

Streicher later claimed that he was only "indirectly responsible" for passage of the anti-Jewish Nuremberg Laws of 1935, and that he felt slighted because he was not directly consulted.

In 1938, Streicher ordered the Great Synagogue of Nuremberg destroyed; he later claimed that his decision was based on his disapproval of its architectural design.

Streicher's excesses brought condemnation even from other Nazis. Streicher's behaviour was viewed as so irresponsible that he alienated much of the party leadership; chief among his enemies in Hitler's hierarchy was *Reichsmarschall* Hermann Göring, who loathed him and later claimed that he forbade his own staff to read *Der Stürmer*.

In spite of his special relationship with Hitler, after 1938 Streicher's position began to unravel. He was accused of keeping Jewish property seized after *Kristallnacht* in November 1938; he was charged with spreading untrue stories about Göring – such as alleging that his daughter Edda was conceived by artificial insemination, and he was confronted with his excessive personal behaviour, including unconcealed adultery, several furious verbal attacks on other *Gauleiter*s and striding through the streets of Nuremberg cracking a bullwhip (this last is portrayed in the 1944 Hollywood film The Hitler Gang). In February 1940 he was stripped of his party offices and withdrew from the public eye, although he was permitted to continue publishing *Der Stürmer*. Streicher also remained on good terms with Hitler.

- C H A P T E R   3 -
HITLER AS AN ORATOR

OPPOSITION TO Hitler came from many quarters and he was not surprised to discover that even among the *völkisch* movement, his popularity was by no means assured. In some quarters Hitler and his followers were despised for their lack of intellectual rigour. For once, Hitler was justified in his suspicions that intellectuals looked down upon him and his movement. The enthusiastic recourse to violence coupled with the mob mentality provoked their justified derision:

"They reproached us bitterly not only for what they called our crude worship of the cudgel but also because, according to them, we had no intellectual forces on our side. These charlatans did not think for a moment that a Demosthenes could be reduced to silence at a mass-meeting by fifty idiots who had come there to shout him down and use their fists against his supporters. The innate cowardice of the pen-and-ink charlatan prevents him from exposing himself to such a danger, for he always works in safe retirement and never dares to make a noise or come forward in public."

One of the many who were drawn to the National Socialist cause at this juncture was Kurt Ludecke. Ludecke, who was later to write an account of his life with Hitler, was a colourful character to say the least. Having been invalided out of the army in 1916 on mental health grounds Ludecke recovered sufficiently to begin a highly successful career as an international businessman. He appears to have been an inveterate deal maker, a mover and shaker with an easy charm which allowed him to access many different social circles. He also appears to have lived life to the full and had an uncanny knack for getting himself into high profile scrapes including being branded as a spy by the French government. For many years the larger than life aspects of Ludecke's 1938 volume

"*I Knew Hitler*" were dismissed as being too imaginative to be true, however in recent years Ludecke has been rehabilitated somewhat and is now seen as a highly credible source by many formerly skeptical historians. Ludecke had befriended Count Reventlow who was an influential figure in *völkisch* circles and in August 1922 Reventlow provided the introduction to Adolf Hitler which would change the course of Ludecke's life for ever. Ludecke's extensive account of hearing Hitler speak is an excellent source in that it provides a comprehensive insight into the circumstances which prevailed in Germany at the time that Hitler was first harbouring thoughts of seizing power by force.

"The final struggle for supremacy among the many would-be dictators had begun; the process of pitiless elimination of the weak was under way. It was deeds, not words, that counted now.

Reventlow suggested that I go with him to Munich, where the political situation was taking on even deeper colour. He had said that he would introduce me to General Ludendorff, and now he

(Left) 'One People, One Empire, One Leader.'
This populist mantra was constantly reinforced by propaganda.
(Right) A poster depicts Hitler as the source of truth.

began to talk also of Dr. Pittinger and of one Adolf Hitler. I had heard that there was an agitator of that name; but, ill-advised by the teacher, I had not tried to meet him. Munich was still the city of charm, but with each visit I found its political aspect more absorbing. The contrast with Berlin was marked; one was the Mecca of Marxists and Jews, the other the citadel of their enemies.

When Reventlow introduced me to Dr. Pittinger, I was warmly received into' the circle of his friends. Here were Colonel Stockhausen, his chief of staff; Count von Soden, the 'chef du cabinet' of Crown Prince Rupprecht; Kahr, the ex-minister; and Poehner, the former police-president. I met many others of their group, and learned much about them, partly through Reventlow's sarcastic tongue. When they proposed appointing me liaison officer for the *Bund Bayern und Reich* between Bavaria and the North, I joined. But it was *faute de mieux*, for I could not escape a vague apprehension that somewhere, in either its personnel or its platform, the *Bund* was too weak for action.

The drastic new laws were threatening the sovereignty of Bavaria, and relations between Berlin and Munich were strained. Within Bavaria itself, two chief political interests were clashing: the Centrist Bavarian Peoples' Party, ready to secede from the Reich if necessary, and the Nationalist *völkisch* element, opposed to any secession. The latter had used Munich, safely so far, as a base for their campaign against Berlin. The Bavarian Government, which was Centrist, was now in the quandary of choosing between surrendering its sovereignty to Berlin or risking an alliance with the *völkisch* Nationalists, which was also against their own interests. Finally they yielded to Berlin, making Bavaria, like the rest of Germany, a hunting-ground for Berlin police seeking the extradition of National activists. The wave of indignation that surged through the land reached its climax in a huge mass demonstration of protest in Munich on 11 August 1922, under the sponsorship of the '*Vaeterlandische Verbaende*,' which was in effect, a holding company loosely co-ordinating all the patriotic

societies, large and small, and including at that time the Nazi Party
- the National Socialist German Workers' Partry.

This was the greatest mass demonstration Munich had ever
seen. It was one of incalculable historical importance, for on that
day a little-known figure stepped into the light as a recognized
public speaker of extraordinary power. This was a man who until
then had literally been snubbed by the higher-ups in the patriotic
societies. Now, because of his growing local importance and for
the sake of a united front, he had been invited to appear as one of
two speakers on a programme in which all were taking part. Adolf
Hitler was scheduled to speak last. It needed no clairvoyance to see
that here was a man who knew how to seize his opportunity. Red
placards announced in huge black letters that he was to appear.
Many who read them had never even heard his name. Here were
inflammatory slogans: 'Versailles: Germany's Ruin... Republic
of the People or State of the Jews?... International Solidarity: A
Jewish World Swindle... Down with the November Criminals...
The National Socialist Movement Must Conquer...'

And every one of his placards ended with the blunt phrase:
'Jews Not Admitted.'

Ludecke went on to recollect the day on which he first heard
Hitler speak to the assembled masses who were there in support
of the various conservative parties and movements which together
constituted the 'Vaeterlandische Verbaende'.

"It was a bright summer day. The Reds had tried their best to
break up the Nazi columns marching through the city, comprising
Storm Troopers followed by sections of the Party. Soon the
assailants were in flight, bruised and beaten, and it had been
demonstrated for, the first time that Nationalists as well as Reds
had the right to march in formation through the streets of Munich,
and that the Nazis were determined to maintain this right.

The 'Patriotic Societies' had assembled without bands and
without flags. 'But when the Nazis marched into the Koenigsplatz
with banners flying, their bands playing stirring German marches,

they were greeted with tremendous cheers. An excited, expectant crowd was now filling the beautiful square to the last inch and overflowing into surrounding streets. There were well over a hundred thousand.

The first speaker, little Dr. Buckeley, harangued this mass in true political fashion. At last he relinquished the platform, and Hitler faced the multitude.

Reventlow had seen to it that we were near the speakers' stand. I was close enough to see Hitler's face, watch every change in his expression, hear every word he said.

When the man stepped forward on the platform, there was almost no applause. He stood silent for a moment. Then he began to speak, quietly and ingratiatingly at first. Before long his voice had risen to a hoarse shriek that gave an extraordinary effect of an intensity of feeling. There were many high-pitched, rasping

(Left) Hitler, our last hope. This rather down beat poster is at odds with the generally positive tone of the typical Nazi propaganda poster.
(Right) In this 1932 poster workers of both brain and hand are urged to join with Hitler the 'front- line soldier'.

notes - Reventlow had told me that his throat had been affected by war-gas - but despite its strident tone, his diction had a distinctly Austrian turn, softer and pleasanter than the German.

Critically I studied this slight, pale man, his brown hair parted on one side and falling again and again over his sweating brow. Threatening and beseeching, with small, pleading hands and flaming, steel-blue eyes, he had the look of a fanatic.

Presently my critical faculty was swept away. Leaning from the tribune as if he were trying to impel his inner self into the consciousness of all these thousands, he was holding the masses, and me with them, under a hypnotic spell by the sheer force of his conviction.

He urged the revival of German honour and manhood with a blast of words that seemed to cleanse. "Bavaria is now the most German land in Germany!" he shouted, to roaring applause. Then, plunging into sarcasm, he indicted the leaders in Berlin

(Left) S.A. Mann Brand, the movie poster advertising the film which was a blatant piece of propaganda.
(Right) An election poster urging the populace to vote list 8 for the Nazis.

30

as 'November Criminals,' daring to put into words thoughts that Germans were now almost afraid to think and certainly to voice.

It was clear that Hitler was feeling the exaltation of the emotional response now surging up toward him from his thousands of hearers. His voice rising to passionate climaxes, he finished his speech with an anthem of hate against the, Novemberlings' and a pledge of undying love for the Fatherland. "Germany must be free!" was his final defiant slogan. Then two last words that were like the sting of a lash:

"Deutschland Erwache!"

Awake, Germany! There was thunderous applause. Then the masses took a solemn oath 'to save Germany in Bavaria from Bolshevism.'

At last the party was at last on the map and Hitler had achieved one of his early goals, the party was by no means the largest, but it was at least being spoken about. Hitler noted with pride that the words 'National Socialist' had become common property and at last signified a definite party programme. The circle of supporters and members was constantly increasing, so that in the winter of 1920-21 the NSDAP were beginning to be taken seriously, at least in Munich. No other conservative party was able to hold large scale mass demonstrations. The cavernous Munich Kindl Hall, which held 5,000 people, was on more than one occasion overcrowded and up till then there was only one other hall, the Krone Circus Hall, into which the NSDAP had not ventured.

- C H A P T E R   4 -

THE CIRCUS KRONE MEETING

ITLER TOOK delight in the ability of his strong arm teams to control increasing levels of violence associated with the NSDAP meetings. He also drew personal satisfaction from the increasing scale of the meetings. The combination of growing public support and the occasional display of physical strength were the two elements which Hitler prized most as his party grew and prospered.

The beer hall brawls and mass meetings were important to Hitler at a personal level. In the autobiographical sections of *Mein Kampf* he records, with obvious pride, a detailed description of four key events which took place during 1921 and 1922. In this respect *Mein Kampf* provides us a pointer to the things that mattered most to Hitler the man and, as such, they provide a unique insight into his inner world. He gives a surprisingly detailed account of the fights, squabbles and rallies which were important to him. On the surface these events are not of enormous significance in themselves and, in the case of the *Schaalsclacht*, the tawdry events which to Hitler seem tumultuous appear to a modern audience as insignificant and petty.

It is only as a result of the large amount of space which Hitler accords to these relatively minor events in *Mein Kampf* that we are alerted to the factors which preoccupied his mind at the time. Had these key events not been highlighted at such length in his book they might otherwise have been overlooked and we would have lost a rare insight into the workings of Hitler's mind.

The initial Circus Krone meeting, held in November 1921, was the first of four events which held great significance for Hitler. In retrospect it fades into insignificance as part of a procession of such events, but we know from *Mein Kampf* that Hitler considered this mass meeting to be his first real personal triumph. It is worth revisiting the events in detail in order to appreciate the weight that Hitler himself attached to otherwise insignificant events.

At the end of January 1921 there were new problems for Germany which led to increased anxiety throughout the country. The main source for concern was Paris Agreement, by which Germany pledged herself to pay the unbelievable sum of a hundred million gold marks, the agreement was due to be confirmed by the allies who had issued the London Ultimatum. To mark the beginning of a popular protest an old-established Munich working committee, representative of various conservative groups, deemed it advisable to call for a public meeting of protest. As a firm opponent of anything connected with Versailles Hitler was anxious that the meeting should be held as soon as possible, but as the days wore on without an announcement Hitler records that he became increasingly nervous and restless as he felt that a lot of time was being wasted and nothing undertaken.

To Hitler's extreme frustration, the organisers continued to dither, finally a meeting was suggested in the Königplatz; but this was turned down by the organizing committee as some members feared the proceedings might be wrecked by Red elements. An alternative suggestion was for a demonstration in front of the sacred Feldherrn Hall which even the forces of reaction would hesitate to profane by violent acts, but this too came to nothing. Finally a combined meeting in the Munich Kindl Hall was suggested and agreed in principle. Meanwhile, day after day had gone by; the big parties had entirely ignored the terrible event, and the working committee could not decide on a definite date for holding the demonstration.

On Tuesday, 1st February 1921, Hitler became increasingly agitated and put forward an urgent demand for a final decision. He was put off until Wednesday 2nd February 1921. On that day Hitler again demanded to be told clearly if and when the meeting was to take place. The reply was again uncertain and evasive, the committee would only vouchsafe that it was 'intended' to arrange a demonstration the following week. At that Hitler lost all patience and in a characteristic fit of pique decided to take matters into his own hands. His gambler's mentality came to the fore and as Fürher of the NSDAP he resolved to conduct a demonstration of protest on his own initiative. At noon on Wednesday 2nd of February 1921 Hitler tells us that he sprang into a frenzy of action and hurriedly dictated the text of the poster and at the same time hired the Krone Circus Hall for the next day, Thursday 3rd February 1921. In those days this was a highly questionable undertaking. Not only because of the uncertainty of filling that vast hall, but also because of the risk of the meeting being wrecked by left wing opponents.

Numerically the growing squad of hall guards was up to the task of policing the Hofbräuhaus, but was not strong enough for such a vast hall as the Circus Krone. Hitler was also uncertain about what to do in case the meeting was broken up as tactically, policing a huge circus building was a different proposition from an ordinary meeting hall. Hitler acknowledge the riskiness of the

(Left) A poster campaigning against the silencing of Hitler during the ban on political speeches. (Right) Hitler depicted as Parsifal with dove of peace descending.

venture and noted that one thing was certain: A failure would destroy the forward momentum which was being built and would throw the NSDAP back into reverse for a long time to come. Hitler knew that if just one meeting was wrecked his playground bully tactics would be exposed and his party's prestige as the proponent of the application superior force would be seriously injured. The floodgates would be opened and his opponents would be encouraged to repeat their success.

To compound the uncertainty Hitler had allowed only one day in which to post the bills advertising the meeting. This was the day of the meeting itself Thursday 3rd February 1921. To add spice to the gamble it rained on the morning of that day and there was genuine reason to fear that many people would prefer to remain at home rather than hurry to a meeting through rain and snow, especially when there was likely to be violence and bloodshed.

In a rare glimpse of self doubt Hitler recorded in *Mein Kampf* how, on that Thursday morning, he was suddenly struck with fear that in the short timescale which he had allowed the hall might not be filled to anything like capacity. He admitted that such a failure would have made him look ridiculous in the eyes of the working committee and his many opponents. However, Hitler was never one to give in easily and faced with the prospect of public humiliation his fear of failure spurred him on to even greater efforts. As the rain turned to sleet Hitler redoubled his efforts and immediately dictated various leaflets, had them printed and distributed that same afternoon.

Hitler knew that it was now a matter of urgent necessity to deliver the message by all means available, and he was sufficiently astute to realize that with time running out extraordinary measures were required. In desperation he resorted to copying the tactics of the Marxist parties which he so despised. Two lorries were hastily hired and were draped as much as possible in red, each had the new NSDAP flag hoisted on it and was then filled with fifteen or twenty members from the party. As the day wore on a desperate series of increasingly frantic orders were given to all available members to canvas the streets as thoroughly and rapidly as possible, to distribute every last leaflet and cajole as many members of the public as possible to attend the mass meeting to be held that very evening. Hitler had stolen the promotional device from his Marxist rivals and he vainly boasted that this was the first time that lorries had driven through the streets bearing flags which were not actually manned by Marxists.

Despite all his best efforts, initially things appeared to have gone badly wrong for Hitler. At seven o'clock in the evening only a few had gathered in the circus hall. In an agony of self doubt Hitler sat at home waiting by the telephone. It must be presumed that if the event was to prove a failure Hitler intended to avoid the personal embarrassment by hiding at home. Hitler records that he was being kept informed by telephone every ten minutes and in an unusual bout of frankness admits that he was becoming uneasy. He knew full well that in the usual scheme of things by seven or a quarter past NSDAP meeting halls were already half filled; sometimes even packed to bursting with the Police struggling to maintain order from those still struggling to gain admission. In their anxiety those reporting to Hitler had entirely forgotten to take into account the huge dimensions of this new meeting place. A thousand people in the Hofbräuhaus was quite an impressive sight, but the same number in the Circus building was simply swallowed up by the sheer scale of the venue. In reality there were for more supporters in attendance than the reports suggested. Shortly afterwards Hitler received more hopeful reports and at a quarter to eight he was informed that the hall was three-quarters filled, with huge crowds still lined up at the pay boxes. It was then that Hitler finally left for the meeting. Hitler arrived at the Circus building at two minutes past eight. There was still a crowd of people outside, partly inquisitive people and many opponents who obviously did not wish to make a contribution to nationalist funds by paying the admission money. They preferred to wait outside and hope for interesting developments for developments.

When Hitler finally entered the great hall of the Circus Krone he records that he felt the same joy he had felt a year previously at the first meeting in the Munich Hofbräu Banquet Hall. It was not until he had forced his way through the solid wall of people and reached the platform that he perceived the full measure of his triumph at which point the feelings of success became overwhelming. To Hitler's delight he saw that the hall was packed to it's limits. More than 5,600 tickets had been sold and, allowing for the unemployed, poor students and the NSDAP's own detachments of men for keeping order, Hitler estimates that a crowd of about 6,500 must have been present.

Rising to the occasion and fuelled by a raging sense of euphoria Hitler began to speak. His theme was 'Future or Downfall' and he recalls how he was filled with joy as he spoke for about two and

(Left) Farmers are soldiers in the fight to smash the British blockade.
(Right) The strong stoic resolve of German women are emphasised in this election poster.

a half hours. From the speaker's platform Hitler had the feeling after the first half-hour that the meeting was going to be a big success. Hitler's speeches typically built very slowly from an almost quiet speaking voice to a manic intensity over the course of a speech which tended to last between two and three hours. After the first hour the speech Hitler recalled that he was already being received by spontaneous outbreaks of applause, but in a departure from the norm after the second hour this died down to a solemn stillness which Hitler boasted would be for ever remembered by all those present. According to his own account nothing broke this imposing silence and only when the last word had been spoken did the meeting give vent to its feelings by spontaneously singing the national anthem. It was a momentous occasion for Hitler, a political breakthrough and a vindication of his increasing belief in his own judgment.

"I watched the scene during the next twenty minutes, as the vast hall slowly emptied itself, and only then did I leave the platform, a happy man, and made my way home."

The events of 3rd February 1921 were one of a series of gambles which informed the growing conviction in Adolf Hitler that he had the ability to make marginal judgment calls. Once again Lucky Linzer had ridden his luck.

A famous series of photographs were taken of the occasion of the first meeting in the Krone Circus Hall. Entitled *Hitler Spricht* (Hitler speaks) the wide shot of the huge crowd bears mute testimony to Hitler's version of events. For Hitler, occupying the centre of his own universe, the meeting had enormous significance.

Hitler's own description of the events is mirrored in the description provided for us by Kurt Ludecke who in the pages of "*I Knew Hitler*" left his own description of a Hitler speech delivered in the fervent hot house atmosphere of Zircus Krone.

"Hitler evidently combined the practical and the spiritual. Counting apparently on the effect of his address in the afternoon, he had arranged for the evening a Nazi meeting in the Zirkus Krone.

The term' Nazi' had been only slightly known up to the hour of his address. Nazi-a sound of a sort that is common in Bavarian speech-is a contraction of the first word of the title of Hitler's party, the '*Nationalsozialistische Deutsche Arbeiter-Partei*.' Now we were hearing these syllables wherever we went in Munich. Reventlow and I found the Zirkus so jammed that there was scarcely room for a pin to drop. Around the platform was grouped a guard of SA - the '*Sturmabteilung*,' husky fellows who looked ready to cope with any situation. I could see the need of them, for it was apparent that the Nazis, more than any others in those days, were daring to assail the Jews, the Communists, the bourgeois round-heads, denouncing what they believed evil. More Storm Troopers encircled the arena and flanked the aisle leading to the tribune. All of them wore red arm-bands bearing the now famous symbol-a black swastika in a white circle.

We were shown to seats reserved for us within a few feet of the platform. In a moment, the expectant murmur of the throng hushed, then ceased. Hitler was entering.

It took courage to risk a second address that day, but the experience of the Koenigsplatz was repeated with even greater intensity, if that was possible. Standing under his own banners, addressing his own followers, Hitler was even more outspoken, flaying the 'system' with that fury of invective of which he is a master and disclosing an extraordinary talent for conveying the most complicated matters in plastic, popular form, comprehensible to anyone.

Again his power was inescapable, gripping and swaying me as it did every one within those walls. Again I had the sensation of surrendering my being to his leadership. When he stopped speaking, his chest still heaving with emotion, there was a moment of dead silence, then a storm of cheers.

Count Reventlow introduced me to Hitler, still perspiring, dishevelled in his dirty trench-coat, his hair plastered against his brow, his face pale, his nostrils distended. Looking closely at him for a long moment, I did not need to wonder where he found the reserves of character and courage that were enabling him to forge ahead of the other leaders. Everything dwelt behind his eyes. We shook hands, and it was arranged that I was to meet him at Nazi headquarters on the following afternoon.

Then his men gathered round him, and the Count and I left. The Zirkus Krone had set the seal on my conversion."

Ludecke may have been won over but the wider world cared somewhat less and after all of his efforts Hitler was outraged when the Munich press reproduced the photographs but reported the meeting as having been merely 'nationalist' in character he was incensed by the fact that they omitted all mention of the NSDAP as promoters of the event.

Despite his frustrations over the lack of anticipated press coverage Hitler sensed that his movement had, for the first time, developed beyond the dimensions of the myriad of tiny *völkisch* parties which littered the Munich scene. At a personal level

(Left) A Waffen SS recruting poster from Munich informs would be volunteers that they may sign up from age seventeen.
(Right) A German Workers Front poster emphasises the idea that workers by hand and brain underpin the strength of the Wehrmacht.

40

however Adolf Hitler was clearly as mesmeric as he was in public and we are fortunate to have this insight into a personal interview with Hitler from the pages of Ludecke's "*I Knew Hitler*".

"At three the next afternoon, I stepped into the open door of what had once been a little *Kaffeehaus* in the Komeliusstrasse, in the poorer section of the city. This was Nazi headquarters. There was a show-window displaying Nazi literature, a large room with a reception corner barred off by a wooden rail, a counter where members paid their dues, a few tables and chairs. That was all, except for two smaller rooms beyond. Hitler took me into one of these and closed the door behind us.

At once I offered myself to him and to his cause without reservation. As frankly as I had talked to Reventlow, I told him the story of my life, dwelling especially upon years during and after the war when I had felt myself baffled at every turn.

Hitler listened closely, studying me keenly, now and then rising from his chair and pacing the floor. I was impressed again by his obvious indifference to his personal appearance; but again I saw that the whole man was concentrated in his eyes, his clear, straightforward, domineering, bright blue eyes.

When I mentioned my appointment in the *Bund Bayern und Reich* he frowned, but approved my suggestion that it might be wise to maintain the collection for a while, to remain vigilant and learn what was going on.

When I rose to leave, it was after seven; we had been talking for over four hours. Solemnly clasping hands, we sealed the pact.

I had given him my soul."

It was clear to Ludecke and thousands like him who had fallen under Hitler's spell that the NSDAP was on the rise could no longer be ignored. With his gambler's instincts now running unchecked Hitler seized the opportunity and, in an effort to dispel any doubt that the meeting was merely an isolated success, he immediately arranged for another meeting at the Zirkus Krone in the following week. The follow up meeting witnessed the same success as the original. Once more the vast hall was overflowing with people. Hitler knew he was on a roll and seized the moment and decided to hold a third meeting during the following week, which also proved a similar success. His speeches were now beginning to form a coherent pattern which struck a rich chord with the conservative and *völkisch* elements. Kurt Ludecke provides a clear impression of how this heady mix of policy and oratory was being received throughout Bavaria.

"Hitler had unfolded a practical programme which would demand the utmost of my strength and ability. I must come down out of the clouds and prepare for intelligent action.

Hitler had accepted me with definite interest; but just the same I was today merely one among less than a thousand inscribed members. Tomorrow would I be helping him to lead, or would I be merely one of those who were led, losing my identity more and more each day as new recruits rallied under the swastika banner?

The Party was young, well-founded; nothing could prevent it from growing, and I was resolved to grow with it. The strength and will were there; I needed only knowledge and opportunity.

During the ensuing weeks I was diligent in learning the ropes, studying the inside structure of the Party, meeting people, reading pertinent literature, discharging whatever duties were given me, and publicizing the Nazi cause and the personality of Hitler wherever I could."

Following these initial successes early in 1921 Hitler records how he increased NSDAP activity in Munich still further. Mass meetings were routinely held once a week, but during some weeks two meetings were held. During midsummer and autumn this increased to three. The NSDAP met regularly at the Circus Hall and it gave Hitler great satisfaction to see that every meeting brought the same measure of success. Ludecke too recorded the phenomenal success of Hitler as a public speaker:

"I do not know how to describe the emotions that swept over

me as I heard this man. His words were like a sacrament. When he spoke of the disgrace of Germany, I felt ready to spring on any enemy. His appeal to German manhood was like a call to arms, the gospel he preached a sacred truth. He seemed another Luther. I forgot everything but the man; then, glancing round, I saw that his magnetism was holding these thousands as one.

Of course I was ripe for this experience. I was a man of thirty-two, weary of disgust and disillusionment, a wanderer seeking a cause; a patriot without a channel for his patriotism, a yearner after the heroic without a hero. The intense will of the man, the passion of his sincerity seemed to flow from him into me. I experienced an exaltation that could be likened only to religious conversion.

I felt sure that no one who had heard Hitler that afternoon could doubt that he was the man of destiny, the vitalizing force in the future of Germany. The masses who had streamed into the Koenigsplatz with a stern sense of national humiliation seemed to be going forth renewed.

(Left) Adolf Hitler is the victor! (Right) Yet another variation on the 'One People, One Empire, One Leader' theme.

The bands struck up, the thousands began to move away. I knew my search was ended. I had found myself, my leader, and my cause."

HITLER ASSUMES CONTROL

Up to the middle of 1921, the intense activity of creating and issuing propaganda and gathering in new followers to the NSDAP was sufficient to fully occupy Hitler and was of immense value to the movement. Hitler devoted two chapters of his 1925/26 work *Mein Kampf*, itself a propaganda tool, to the study and practice of propaganda. He claimed to have learnt the value of propaganda as a World War I infantryman exposed to very effective British and ineffectual German propaganda. The argument that Germany lost the war largely because of British propaganda efforts, expounded at length in *Mein Kampf*, reflected then common German nationalist claims. Although untrue – German propaganda during World War I was mostly more advanced than that of the British – it became the official truth of Nazi Germany thanks to its reception by Hitler.

Mein Kampf contains the blueprint of later Nazi propaganda efforts. Assessing his audience, Hitler writes in chapter VI:

"Propaganda must always address itself to the broad masses of the people. (...) All propaganda must be presented in a popular form and must fix its intellectual level so as not to be above the heads of the least intellectual of those to whom it is directed. (...) The art of propaganda consists precisely in being able to awaken the imagination of the public through an appeal to their feelings, in finding the appropriate psychological form that will arrest the attention and appeal to the hearts of the national masses. The broad masses of the people are not made up of diplomats or professors of public jurisprudence nor simply of persons who are able to form reasoned judgment in given cases, but a vacillating crowd of human children who are constantly wavering between one idea and another. (...) The great majority of a nation is so feminine in its character and outlook that its thought and conduct are ruled by sentiment rather than by sober reasoning. This sentiment, however, is not complex, but simple and consistent. It is not highly differentiated, but has only the negative and positive notions of love and hatred, right and wrong, truth and falsehood.

As to the methods to be employed, he explains:

"Propaganda must not investigate the truth objectively and, in so far as it is favourable to the other side, present it according to the theoretical rules of justice; yet it must present only that aspect of the truth which is favourable to its own side. (...) The receptive powers of the masses are very restricted, and their understanding is feeble. On the other hand, they quickly forget. Such being the case, all effective propaganda must be confined to a few bare essentials and those must be expressed as far as possible in stereotyped formulas. These slogans should be persistently repeated until the very last individual has come to grasp the idea that has been put forward. (...) Every change that is made in the subject of a propagandist message must always emphasize the same conclusion. The leading slogan must of course be illustrated in many ways and from several angles, but in the end one must always return to the assertion of the same formula."

Hitler put these ideas into practice with the reestablishment of the *Völkischer Beobachter*, a daily newspaper published by the Nazi Party (NSDAP) from February 1925 on, whose circulation reached 26, 175 in 1929. It was joined in 1926 by Joseph Goebbels's *Der Angriff*, another unabashedly and crudely propagandistic paper.

- CHAPTER 5 -
ENTER DR. GOEBBELS

URING MOST of the Nazis' time in opposition, their means of propaganda remained limited. With little access to mass media, the party continued to rely heavily on Hitler and a few others speaking at public meetings until 1929. In April 1930, Hitler appointed Goebbels head of party propaganda. Goebbels, a former journalist and Nazi party officer in Berlin, soon proved his skills. Among his first successes was the organization of riotous demonstrations that succeeded in having the American anti-war film All Quiet on the Western Front banned in Germany.

Goebbels was born in Rheydt, an industrial town south of Mönchengladbach on the edge of the Ruhr district. His family were Catholics; his father was a factory clerk, his mother originally a farmhand. Goebbels had four siblings: Hans (1893–1947), Konrad (1895–1949), Elisabeth (1901–1915) and Maria (born 1910, later married to the German filmmaker Max W. Kimmich). He was educated at a Christian Gymnasium, where he completed his *Abitur* (university entrance examination) in 1916. He had a deformed right leg, the result either of club foot or osteomyelitis. William L. Shirer, who worked in Berlin as a journalist in the 1930s and was acquainted with Goebbels, wrote in The Rise and Fall of the Third Reich (1960) that the deformity was from a childhood attack of osteomyelitis and a failed operation to correct it. Goebbels wore a metal brace and special shoe because of his shortened leg, but nevertheless walked with a limp. He was rejected for military service in World War I, which he bitterly resented. He later sometimes misrepresented himself as a war veteran and his disability as a war wound. He did act as an "office soldier" from June to October 1917 in Rheydt's "Patriotic Help Unit".

Goebbels attended the boarding school of German Franciscan brothers in Bleijerheide, Kerkrade in the Netherlands. Gradually losing his Catholic faith he studied literature and philosophy at the universities of Bonn, Würzburg, Freiburg and Heidelberg, where he wrote his doctoral thesis on a minor 19th century romantic dramatist, Wilhelm von Schütz. His two most influential teachers,

Goebbels, German Federal Archive photo.

Friedrich Gundolf and his doctoral supervisor at Heidelberg, Max Freiherr von Waldberg, were Jews. His intelligence and political astuteness were generally acknowledged even by his enemies.

After completing his doctorate in 1921, Goebbels worked as a journalist and tried for several years to become a published author. He wrote a semi-autobiographical novel, Michael, two verse plays, and quantities of romantic poetry. In these works, he revealed the psychological damage his physical limitations (having a clubbed foot, and, in a lesser sense being so far from the Aryan ideal, having brown eyes and dark brown hair and standing at only 5'5) had caused. "The very name of the hero, Michael, to whom he gave many autobiographical features, suggests the way his self-identification was pointing: a figure of light, radiant, tall, unconquerable," and above all "'To be a soldier! To stand sentinel! One ought always to be a soldier,' wrote Michael-Goebbels." Goebbels found another form of compensation in the pursuit of women, a lifelong compulsion he indulged "with extraordinary vigor and a surprising degree of success." His diaries reveal a long succession of affairs, before and after his marriage before a Protestant pastor in 1931 to Magda Quandt, with whom he had six children.

Goebbels was embittered by the frustration of his literary career; his novel did not find a publisher until 1929 and his plays were never staged. He found an outlet for his desire to write in his diaries, which he began in 1923 and continued for the rest of his life. He later worked as a bank clerk and a caller on the stock exchange. During this period, he read avidly and formed his political views. Major influences were Friedrich Nietzsche, Oswald Spengler and, most importantly, Houston Stewart Chamberlain, the British-born German writer who was one of the founders of "scientific" anti-Semitism, and whose book The Foundations of the Nineteenth Century (1899) was one of the standard works of the extreme right in Germany. Goebbels spent the winter of 1919–20 in Munich, where he witnessed and admired the violent nationalist reaction against the attempted communist revolution in Bavaria. His first political hero was Anton Graf von Arco auf Valley, the man who assassinated the Bavarian prime minister Kurt Eisner. Hitler was in Munich at the same time and entered politics as a result of similar experiences.

The culture of the German extreme right was violent and anti-intellectual, which posed a challenge to the physically frail University graduate. Joachim Fest writes:

"This was the source of his hatred of the intellect, which was a form of self-hatred, his longing to degrade himself, to submerge himself in the ranks of the masses, which ran curiously parallel with his ambition and his tormenting need to distinguish himself. He was incessantly tortured by the fear of being regarded as a 'bourgeois intellectual'... It always seemed as if he were offering blind devotion (to Nazism) to make up for his lack of all those characteristics of the racial elite which nature had denied him."

The Guarantors of German military strength depicted as the Heer and SA.

NAZI ACTIVIST

Like others who were later prominent in the Third Reich, Goebbels came into contact with the Nazi Party in 1923, during the campaign of resistance to the French occupation of the Ruhr. Hitler's imprisonment following the failed November 1923 "Beer Hall Putsch" left the party temporarily leaderless, and when the 27-year-old Goebbels joined the party in late 1924 the most important influence on his political development was Gregor Strasser, who became Nazi organizer in northern Germany in March 1924. Strasser ("the most able of the leading Nazis" of this period) took the "socialist" component of National Socialism far more seriously than did Hitler and other members of the Bavarian leadership of the party.

"National and socialist! What goes first, and what comes afterwards?" Goebbels asked rhetorically in a debate with Theodor Vahlen, *Gauleiter* (regional party head) of Pomerania, in the Rhineland party newspaper *National-sozialistische Briefe* (National-Socialist Letters), of which he was editor, in mid-1925. "With us in the west, there can be no doubt. First socialist redemption, then comes national liberation like a whirlwind... Hitler stands between both opinions, but he is on his way to coming over to us completely." Goebbels, with his journalistic skills, thus soon became a key ally of Strasser in his struggle with the Bavarians over the party program. The conflict was not, so they thought, with Hitler, but with his lieutenants, Rudolf Hess, Julius Streicher and Hermann Esser, who, they said, were mismanaging the party in Hitler's absence. In 1925, Goebbels published an open letter to "my friends of the left," urging unity between socialists and Nazis against the capitalists. "You and I," he wrote, "we are fighting one another although we are not really enemies."

In February 1926, Hitler, having finished working on *Mein Kampf*, made a sudden return to party affairs and soon disabused the northerners of any illusions about where he stood. He summoned about 60 *Gauleiter*s and other activists, including Goebbels, to a meeting at Bamberg, in Streicher's *Gau* of Franconia, where he gave a two-hour speech repudiating the political program of the "socialist" wing of the party. For Hitler, the real enemy of the German people was always the Jews, not the capitalists.

Goebbels speaking at a rally against the Lausanne Conference (1932).

Goebbels was bitterly disillusioned. "I feel devastated," he wrote. "What sort of Hitler? A reactionary?" He was horrified by Hitler's characterization of socialism as "a Jewish creation", his declaration that the Soviet Union must be destroyed, and his assertion that private property would not be expropriated by a Nazi government. "I no longer fully believe in Hitler. That's the terrible thing: my inner support has been taken away."

Hitler, however, recognized Goebbels' talents. In April, he brought Goebbels to Munich, sending his own car to meet him at the railway station, and gave him a long private audience. Hitler berated Goebbels over his support for the "socialist" line, but offered to "wipe the slate clean" if Goebbels would now accept his leadership. Goebbels capitulated completely, offering Hitler his total loyalty – a pledge that was clearly sincere, and that he adhered to until the end of his life. "I love him... He has thought through everything," Goebbels wrote. "Such a sparkling mind can be my leader. I bow to the greater one, the political genius". Later he wrote: "Adolf Hitler, I love you because you are both great and simple at the same time. What one calls a genius." Fest writes:

From this point on he submitted himself, his whole existence, to his attachment to the person of the Führer, consciously eliminating all inhibitions springing from intellect, free will and self-respect. Since this submission was an act less of faith than of insight, it stood firm through all vicissitudes to the end. 'He who forsakes the Führer withers away,' he would later write.

PROPAGANDIST IN BERLIN

In October 1926, Hitler rewarded Goebbels for his new loyalty by making him the party "*Gauleiter*" for the Berlin section of the National Socialists. Goebbels was then able to use the new position to indulge his literary aspirations in the German capital, which he perceived to be a stronghold of the socialists and communists.

Here, Goebbels discovered his talent as a propagandist, writing such tracts as 1926's The Second Revolution and Lenin or Hitler.

Here, he was also able to indulge his heretofore latent taste for violence, if only vicariously through the actions of the street fighters under his command. History, he said, "is made in the street," and he was determined to challenge the dominant parties of the left – the Social Democrats and Communists – in the streets of Berlin. Working with the local S.A. (stormtrooper) leaders, he deliberately provoked beer-hall battles and street brawls, frequently involving firearms. "Beware, you dogs," he wrote to his former "friends of the left": "When the Devil is loose in me you will not curb him again." When the inevitable deaths occurred, he exploited them for the maximum effect, turning the street fighter Horst Wessel, who was killed at his home by enemy political activists, into a martyr and hero.

In Berlin, Goebbels was able to give full expression to his genius for propaganda, as editor of the Berlin Nazi newspaper *Der Angriff* (The Attack) and as the author of a steady stream of Nazi posters and handbills. "He rose within a few months to be the city's most feared agitator." His propaganda techniques were totally cynical: "That propaganda is good which leads to success, and that is bad which fails to achieve the desired result," he wrote. "It is not propaganda's task to be intelligent, its task is to lead to success."

Among his favourite targets were socialist leaders such as Hermann Müller and Carl Severing, and the Jewish Berlin Police President, Bernhard Weiß (1880–1951), whom he subjected to a relentless campaign of Jew-baiting in the hope of provoking a crackdown he could then exploit. The Social Democrat city government obliged in 1927 with an eight-month ban on the party, which Goebbels exploited to the limit. When a friend criticized him for denigrating Weiss, a man with an exemplary military record, "he explained cynically that he wasn't in the least interested in Weiss, only in the propaganda effect."

Goebbels also discovered a talent for oratory, and was soon second in the Nazi movement only to Hitler as a public speaker. Where Hitler's style was hoarse and passionate, Goebbels' was cool, sarcastic and often humorous: he was a master of biting invective and insinuation, although he could whip himself into a rhetorical frenzy if the occasion demanded. Unlike Hitler, however, he retained a cynical detachment from his own rhetoric. He openly acknowledged that he was exploiting the lowest instincts of the German people – racism, xenophobia, class envy and insecurity. He could, he said, play the popular will like a piano, leading the masses wherever he wanted them to go. "He drove his listeners into ecstasy, making them stand up, sing songs, raise their arms, repeat

Goebbels with Leni Riefenstahl in 1937.

oaths – and he did it, not through the passionate inspiration of the moment, but as the result of sober psychological calculation."

Goebbels' words and actions made little impact on the political loyalties of Berlin. At the 1928 Reichstag elections, the Nazis polled less than 2% of the vote in Berlin compared with 33% for the Social Democrats and 25% for the Communists. At this election Goebbels was one of the 10 Nazis elected to the Reichstag, which brought him a salary of 750 Reichsmarks a month and immunity from prosecution. Even when the impact of the Great Depression led to an enormous surge in support for the Nazis across Germany, Berlin resisted the party's appeal more than any other part of Germany: at its peak in 1932, the Nazi Party polled 28% in Berlin to the combined left's 55%. But his outstanding talents, and the obvious fact that he stood high in Hitler's regard, earned Goebbels the grudging respect of the anti-intellectual brawlers of the Nazi movement, who called him "our little doctor" with a mixture of affection and amusement. By 1928, still aged only 31, he was acknowledged to be one of the inner circle of Nazi leaders. "The S.A. would have let itself be hacked to bits for him," wrote Horst Wessel in 1929.

The Great Depression led to a new resurgence of "left" sentiment in some sections of the Nazi Party, led by Gregor Strasser's brother Otto, who argued that the party ought to be competing with the Communists for the loyalties of the unemployed and the industrial workers by promising to expropriate the capitalists. Hitler, whose dislike of working class militancy reflected his social origins in the small-town lower middle class, was thoroughly opposed to this line. He recognized that the growth in Nazi support at the 1930 elections had mainly come from the middle class and from farmers, and he was now busy building bridges to the upper middle classes and to German business. In April 1930, he fired Strasser as head of the Nazi Party national propaganda apparatus and appointed Goebbels to replace him, giving him control of the party's national newspaper, the *Völkischer Beobachter* (People's

Observer), as well as other Nazi papers across the country. Goebbels, although he continued to show "leftish" tendencies in some of his actions (such as co-operating with the Communists in supporting the Berlin transport workers' strike in November 1932), was totally loyal to Hitler in his struggle with the Strassers, which culminated in Otto's expulsion from the party in July 1930.

Despite his revolutionary rhetoric, Goebbels' most important contribution to the Nazi cause between 1930 and 1933 was as the organizer of successive election campaigns: The Reichstag elections of September 1930, July and November 1932 and March 1933, and Hitler's presidential campaign of March–April 1932. He proved to be an organizer of genius, choreographing Hitler's dramatic airplane tours of Germany and pioneering the use of radio and cinema for electoral campaigning. The Nazi Party's use of torchlight parades, brass bands, massed choirs, and similar techniques caught the imagination of many voters, particularly young people. "His propaganda headquarters in Munich sent out a constant stream of directives to local and regional party sections, often providing fresh slogans and fresh material for the campaign." Although the spectacular rise in the Nazi vote in 1930 and July 1932 was caused mainly by the effects of the Depression, Goebbels as party campaign manager was naturally given much of the credit.

PROPAGANDA MINISTER

"Personally he likes nobody, is liked by nobody, runs the most efficient Nazi department." - Life, 28 March 1938

When Hitler was appointed Reich Chancellor of Germany on 30 January 1933, Goebbels was initially given no office: the coalition cabinet Hitler headed contained only a minority of Nazis as part of the deal he had negotiated with President Paul von Hindenburg and the conservative parties. However, as the propaganda head of the ruling party, a party with no great respect for the law, he immediately behaved as though he were in power. He commandeered the state radio to produce a live broadcast of the torchlight parade that celebrated Hitler's assumption of office. On 13 March, Goebbels had his reward for his part in bringing the Nazis to power by being appointed Reich Minister of Public Enlightenment and Propaganda (*Volksaufklärung und Propaganda*), with a seat in the Cabinet.

The role of the new ministry, which took over palatial accommodation in the 18th-century Leopold Palace on Wilhelmstrasse, just across from Hitler's offices in the Reich Chancellery, was to centralize Nazi control of all aspects of German cultural and intellectual life, particularly the press, radio and the visual and performing arts. On 1 May, Goebbels organised the massive demonstrations and parades to mark the "Day of National Labour," which preceded the Nazi takeover and destruction of the German trade union movement. By 3 May, he was able to boast

(Left) Comrade worker you fight with us. Celebrate your craft.
(Right) We are for Hitler! This election poster depicts the typical workforce standing squarely behind Adolf Hitler.

in his diary: "We are the masters of Germany." On 10 May, he supervised an even more symbolic event in the establishment of Nazi cultural power: the burning of up to 20,000 books by Jewish or anti-Nazi authors in the *Opernplatz* next to the university.

The hegemonic ambitions of the Propaganda Ministry were shown by the divisions Goebbels soon established: Press, radio, film, theatre, music, literature, and publishing. In each of these, a *Reichskammer* (Reich Chamber) was established, co-opting leading figures from the field (usually not known Nazis) to head each Chamber, and requiring them to supervise the purge of Jews, socialists and liberals, as well as practitioners of "degenerate" art forms such as abstract art and atonal music. The respected composer Richard Strauss, for example, became head of the Reich Music Chamber. Goebbels' orders were backed by the threat of force. The many prominent Jews in the arts and the mass media emigrated in large numbers rather than risk the fists of the SA and the gates of the concentration camp, as did many socialists and liberals. Some non-Jewish anti-Nazis with good connections or international reputations survived until the mid-1930s, but most were forced out sooner or later.

Control of the arts and media was not just a matter of personnel. Soon the content of every newspaper, book, novel, play, film, broadcast and concert, from the level of nationally-known publishers and orchestras to local newspapers and village choirs, was subject to supervision by the Propaganda Ministry, although a process of self-censorship was soon effectively operating in all these fields, leaving the Ministry in Berlin free to concentrate on the most politically sensitive areas such as major newspapers and the state radio. In his 1933 speech, "Radio as the Eighth Great Power" he said:

We... intend a principled transformation in the world view of our entire society, a revolution of the greatest possible extent that will leave nothing out, changing the life of our nation in every regard... It would not have been possible for us to take power or to use it in the ways we have without the radio and the airplane. It is no exaggeration to say that the German revolution, at least in the form it took, would have been impossible without the airplane and the radio.

No author could publish, no painter could exhibit, no singer could broadcast, no critic could criticize, unless they were a member of the appropriate Reich Chamber, and membership was conditional on good behaviour. Goebbels could bribe as well as threaten: he secured a large budget for his Ministry, with which he was able to offer generous salaries and subsidies to those in the arts who co-operated with him. Most artists, theatres, and orchestras - after struggling to survive the Depression - found these inducements hard to refuse.

As one of the most highly educated members of the Nazi leadership, and the one with the most authentic pretensions to high culture, Goebbels was sensitive to charges that he was dragging German culture down to the level of mere propaganda. He responded by saying that the purpose of both art and propaganda was to bring about a spiritual mobilization of the German people.

Goebbels insisted that German high culture must be allowed to carry on, both for reasons of international prestige and to win the loyalty of the upper middle classes, who valued art forms such as opera and the symphony. He thus became to some extent the protector of the arts as well as their regulator. In this, he had the support of Hitler, a passionate devotee of Richard Wagner. But Goebbels always had to bow to Hitler's views. Hitler loathed modernism of all kinds, and Goebbels (whose own tastes were sympathetic to modernism) was forced to acquiesce in imposing very traditionalist forms on the artistic and musical worlds. The music of Paul Hindemith, for example, was banned simply because Hitler did not like it.

Goebbels also resisted the complete Nazification of the arts because he knew that the masses must be allowed some respite from slogans and propaganda. He ensured that film studios such as UFA at Babelsberg near Berlin continued to produce a stream of comedies and light romances, which drew mass audiences to the cinema where they would also watch propaganda newsreels and Nazi epics. His abuse of his position as Propaganda Minister and the reputation that built up around his use of the casting couch was well known. Many actresses wrote later of how Goebbels had tried to lure them to his home. He acquired the nickname "*Bock von Babelsberg*" lit: "*Babelsberg Stud*". He resisted considerable pressure to ban all foreign films – helped by the fact that Hitler sometimes watched foreign films. For the same reason, Goebbels worked to bring culture to the masses – promoting the sale of cheap radios, organizing free concerts in factories, staging art exhibitions in small towns and establishing mobile cinemas to bring the movies to every village. All of this served short-term propaganda ends, but also served to reconcile the German people, particularly the working class, to the regime.

(Left) A poster advertising the documentary film, 'The Eternal Jew.'
(Right) This election poster promises that Judeo-Marxist vermin will be cleared from Sachsen by the will of the streotypical Aryan labourer.

In October 1941 Goebbels organized the *"Weimarer Dichtertreffen"* (Weimar Convention of Poets) inviting collaborating writers from all of Europe. Under Goebbels auspices the participating members (e.g. Pierre Drieu La Rochelle and Robert Brasillach) founded the *"Europäische Schriftstellervereinigung"* (European Writers' League), officially in March 1942. Hans Carossa was president, Giovanni Papini vice president.

GOEBBELS AND THE JEWS

Despite the enormous power of the Propaganda Ministry over German cultural life, Goebbels' status began to decline once the Nazi regime was firmly established in power. This was because the real business of the Nazi regime was preparation for war, and although propaganda was a part of this, it was not the primary objective. By the mid-1930s, Hitler's most powerful subordinates were Hermann Göring, as head of the Four Year Plan for crash rearmament, and Heinrich Himmler, head of the SS and police apparatus. Once the internal enemies of the Nazi Party were destroyed, as they effectively were by 1935, Goebbels' propaganda efforts began to lose their point, and without an enemy to fight, his rhetoric began to sound hollow and unconvincing.

As a man of education and culture, Goebbels had once mocked the "primitive" anti-Semitism of Nazis such as Julius Streicher. But as Joachim Fest observes: "Goebbels (found) in the increasingly unrestrained practice of anti-Semitism by the state new possibilities into which he threw himself with all the zeal of an ambitious man worried by a constant diminution of his power." Fest also suggests a psychological motive: "A man who conformed so little to the National Socialist image of the elite… may have had his reason, in the struggles for power at Hitler's court, for offering keen anti-Semitism as a counterweight to his failure to conform to a type." Whatever his motives, Goebbels took every opportunity to attack the Jews. From 1933 onwards, he was bracketed with Streicher among the regime's most virulent anti-Semites. "Some people think," he told a Berlin rally in June 1935, "that we haven't noticed how the Jews are trying once again to spread themselves over all our streets. The Jews ought to please observe the laws of hospitality and not behave as if they were the same as us."

The sarcastic "humour" of Goebbels' speeches did not conceal the reality of his threat to the Jews. In his capacity as *Gauleiter* of Berlin, and thus as de facto ruler of the capital (although there was still officially an *Oberbürgermeister* and city council), Goebbels maintained constant pressure on the city's large Jewish community, forcing them out of business and professional life and placing obstacles in the way of their being able to live normal lives, such as banning them from public transport and city facilities. There was some respite during 1936, while Berlin hosted the Olympic Games, but from 1937 the intensity of his anti-Semitic words and actions began to increase again. "The Jews must get out of Germany, indeed out of Europe altogether," he wrote in his diary in November 1937. "That will take some time, but it must and will happen." By mid-1938 Goebbels was investigating the possibility of requiring all Jews to wear an identifying mark and of confining them to a ghetto, but these were ideas whose time had not yet come. "Aim – drive the Jews out of Berlin," he wrote in his diary in June 1938, "and without any sentimentality."

In November 1938, Goebbels got the chance to take decisive action against the Jews for which he had been waiting when a Jewish youth, Herschel Grynszpan, shot a German diplomat in Paris, Ernst vom Rath, in revenge for the deportation of his family to Poland and the persecution of German Jews generally. On 9 November, the evening vom Rath died of his wounds, Goebbels was at the Bürgerbräu Keller in Munich with Hitler, celebrating the anniversary of the 1923 Beer Hall Putsch with a large crowd of veteran Nazis. Goebbels told Hitler that "spontaneous" anti-Jewish violence had already broken out in

German cities, although in fact this was not true: this was a clear case of Goebbels manipulating Hitler for his own ends. When Hitler said he approved of what was happening, Goebbels took this as authorization to organize a massive, nationwide pogrom against the Jews. He wrote in his diary:

"(Hitler) decides: demonstrations should be allowed to continue. The police should be withdrawn. For once the Jews should get the feel of popular anger... I immediately gave the necessary instructions to the police and the Party. Then I briefly spoke in that vein to the Party leadership. Stormy applause. All are instantly at the phones. Now people will act."

The result of Goebbels' incitement was *Kristallnacht*, the "Night of Broken Glass," during which the S.A. and Nazi Party went on a rampage of anti-Jewish violence and destruction, killing at least 90 and maybe as many as 200 people, destroying over a thousand

(Left) An election poster from the early 1930s proclaims the Nazis as the party who will deliver freedom and bread. (Right) Stuka dive bombers are depicted at work over a bomb ravaged English city. The tables were soon to be turned however and the consequences were brought horrifyingly to life at Hamburg and Dresden.

synagogues and hundreds of Jewish businesses and homes, and dragging some 30,000 Jews off to concentration camps, where at least another thousand died before the remainder were released after several months of brutal treatment. The longer-term effect was to drive 80,000 Jews to emigrate, most leaving behind all their property in their desperation to escape. Foreign opinion reacted with horror, bringing to a sudden end the climate of appeasement of Nazi Germany in the western democracies. Goebbels' pogrom thus moved Germany significantly closer to war, at a time when rearmament was still far from complete. Göring and some other Nazi leaders were furious at Goebbels' actions, about which they had not been consulted. Goebbels, however, was delighted. "As was to be expected, the entire nation is in uproar," he wrote. "This is one dead man who is costing the Jews dear. Our darling Jews will think twice in future before gunning down German diplomats." In 1942 Goebbels was involved in the deportation of Berlin's Jews.

MAN OF POWER

These events were well-timed from the point of view of Goebbels' relations with Hitler. In 1937, he had begun an intense affair with the Czech actress Lída Baarová, causing the break-up of her marriage. When Magda Goebbels learned of this affair in October 1938, she complained to Hitler, a conservative in sexual matters who was fond of Magda and the Goebbels' young children. He ordered Goebbels to break off his affair, whereupon Goebbels offered his resignation, which Hitler refused. On 15 October, Goebbels attempted suicide. A furious Hitler then ordered Himmler to remove Baarová from Germany, and she was deported to Czechoslovakia, from where she later left for Italy. These events damaged Goebbels' standing with Hitler, and his zeal in furthering Hitler's anti-Semitic agenda was in part an effort to restore his reputation. The Baarová affair, however, did nothing to dampen Goebbels' enthusiasm for womanizing. As late as 1943, the Hitler Youth leader Artur Axmann was ingratiating himself with Goebbels by procuring young women for him.

Goebbels, like all the Nazi leaders, could not afford to defy Hitler's will in matters of this kind. By 1938, they had all become wealthy men, but their wealth was dependent on Hitler's continuing goodwill and willingness to turn a blind eye to their corruption. Until the Nazis came to power, Goebbels had been a relatively poor man, and his main income was the salary of 750 Reichsmarks a month he had gained by election to the Reichstag in 1928. By 1936, although he was not nearly as corrupt as some other senior Nazis, such as Göring and Robert Ley, Goebbels was earning 300,000 Reichsmarks a year in "fees" for writing in his own newspaper, *Der Angriff* (The Attack), as well as his ministerial salary and many other sources of income. These payments were in effect bribes from the papers' publisher Max Amann. He owned a villa on Schwanenwerder island and another at Bogensee near Wandlitz in Brandenburg, which he spent 2.3 million Reichsmarks refurbishing. The tax office, as it did for all the Nazi leaders, gave him generous exemptions.

Whatever the loss of real power suffered by Goebbels during the middle years of the Nazi regime, he remained one of Hitler's intimates. Since his offices were close to the Chancellery, he was a frequent guest for lunch, during which he became adept at listening to Hitler's monologues and agreeing with his opinions. In the months leading up to the war, his influence began to increase again. He ranked along with Joachim von Ribbentrop, Göring, Himmler, and Martin Bormann as the senior Nazi with the most access to Hitler, which in an autocratic regime meant access to power. The fact that Hitler was fond of Magda Goebbels and the children also gave Goebbels entrée to Hitler's inner circle. The Goebbels family regularly visited Hitler's Bavarian mountain retreat, the Berghof. But, he was not kept directly informed of military and diplomatic developments, relying on second-hand accounts to hear what Hitler was doing.

GOEBBELS AT WAR

In the years 1936 to 1939, Hitler, while professing his desire for peace, led Germany firmly and deliberately towards a confrontation. Goebbels was one of the most enthusiastic proponents of aggressively pursuing Germany's territorial claims sooner rather than later, along with Himmler and Foreign Minister von Ribbentrop. He saw it as his job to make the German people accept this and if possible welcome it. At the time of the Sudetenland crisis in 1938, Goebbels was well aware that the great majority of Germans did not want a war, and used every propaganda resource at his disposal to overcome what he called this "war psychosis," by whipping up sympathy for the Sudeten Germans and hatred of the Czechs. After the western powers acceded to Hitler's demands concerning Czechoslovakia in 1938, Goebbels soon redirected his propaganda machine against Poland. From May onwards, he orchestrated a "hate campaign" against Poland, fabricating stories about atrocities against ethnic Germans in Danzig and other cities. Even so, he was unable to persuade the majority of Germans to welcome the prospect of war.

Once war began in September 1939, Goebbels began a steady process of extending his influence over domestic policy. After 1940, Hitler made few public appearances, and even his broadcasts became less frequent, so Goebbels increasingly became the face and the voice of the Nazi regime for the German people. With Hitler preoccupied with the war, Himmler focusing on the "final solution to the Jewish question" in eastern Europe, and with Hermann Göring's position declining with the failure of the German Air Force (*Luftwaffe*), Goebbels sensed a power vacuum in domestic policy and moved to fill it. Since civilian morale was his responsibility, he increasingly concerned himself with matters such as wages, rationing and housing, which affected morale and therefore productivity. He came to see the lethargic and demoralized Göring, still Germany's economic supremo as head of the Four Year Plan Ministry, as his main enemy. To undermine Göring, he forged an alliance with Himmler, although the SS chief remained wary of him. A more useful ally was Albert Speer, a Hitler favourite who was appointed Armaments Minister in February 1942. Goebbels and Speer worked through 1942 to persuade Hitler to dismiss Göring as economic head and allow the domestic economy to be run by a revived Cabinet headed by themselves.

However, in February 1943, the crushing German defeat at the Battle of Stalingrad produced a crisis in the regime. Goebbels was forced to ally himself with Göring to thwart a bid for power by Bormann, head of the Nazi Party Chancellery and Secretary to the Führer. Bormann exploited the disaster at Stalingrad, and his daily access to Hitler, to persuade him to create a three-man junta representing the State, the Army, and the Party, represented

(Left) The theme of building a new Germany by hard work under the direction of Hitler is evident in this propaganda poster. (Right) A poster advertising the National Socialist Association old War Veterans.

respectively by Hans Lammers, head of the Reich Chancellery, Field Marshal Wilhelm Keitel, chief of the OKW (armed forces high command), and Bormann, who controlled the Party and access to the Führer. This Committee of Three would exercise dictatorial powers over the home front. Goebbels, Speer, Göring and Himmler all saw this proposal as a power grab by Bormann and a threat to their power, and combined to block it.

However, their alliance was shaky at best. This was mainly because during this period Himmler was still cooperating with Bormann to gain more power at the expense of Göring and most of the traditional Reich administration; Göring's loss of power had resulted in an overindulgence in the trappings of power and his strained relations with Goebbels made it difficult for a unified coalition to be formed, despite the attempts of Speer and Göring's *Luftwaffe* deputy Field Marshal Erhard Milch, to reconcile the two Party comrades.

Goebbels instead tried to persuade Hitler to appoint Göring as head of the government. His proposal had a certain logic, as Göring – despite the failures of the *Luftwaffe* and his own corruption – was still very popular among the German people, whose morale was waning since Hitler barely appeared in public since the defeat at Stalingrad. However, this proposal was increasingly unworkable given Göring's increasing incapacity and, more importantly, Hitler's increasing contempt for him due to his blaming of Göring for Germany's defeats. This was a measure by Hitler designed to deflect criticism from himself.

The result was that nothing was done – the Committee of Three declined into irrelevance due to the loss of power by Keitel and Lammers and the ascension of Bormann and the situation continued to drift, with administrative chaos increasingly undermining the war effort. The ultimate responsibility for this lay with Hitler, as Goebbels well knew, referring in his diary to a "crisis of leadership", but Goebbels was too much under Hitler's spell ever to challenge his power.

Goebbels launched a new offensive to place himself at the centre of policy-making. On 18 February, he delivered a passionate "Total War Speech" at the Sports Palace in Berlin. Goebbels demanded from his audience a commitment to "total war," the complete mobilization of the German economy and German society for the war effort. To motivate the German people to continue the struggle, he cited three theses as the basis of this argument:

1. If the German Armed Forces (Wehrmacht) were not in a position to break the danger from the Eastern front, then Nazi Germany would fall to Bolshevism, and all of Europe would fall shortly afterward;

2. The German Armed Forces, the German people, and the Axis Powers alone had the strength to save Europe from this threat;

3. Danger was a motivating force. Germany had to act quickly and decisively, or it would be too late.

Goebbels concluded that "Two thousand years of Western history are in danger." He blamed Germany's failures on the Jews.

Sports Palace speech.

Goebbels hoped in this way to persuade Hitler to give him and his ally Speer control of domestic policy for a program of total commitment to arms production and full labour conscription, including women. But Hitler, supported by Göring, resisted these demands, which he feared would weaken civilian morale and lead to a repetition of the debacle of 1918, when the German army had been undermined (in Hitler's view) by a collapse of the home front. Nor was Hitler willing to allow Goebbels or anyone else to usurp his own power as the ultimate source of all decisions. Goebbels privately lamented "a complete lack of direction in German domestic policy," but of course he could not directly criticize Hitler or go against his wishes.

GOEBBELS AND THE HOLOCAUST

Heinrich Himmler, one of the main architects of the Holocaust, preferred that the matter not be discussed in public. Despite this, in an editorial in *Das Reich* in November 1941 Goebbels quoted Hitler's 1939 "prophecy" that the Jews would be the loser in the coming world war. Now, he said, Hitler's prophecy was coming true: "Jewry," he said, "is now suffering the gradual process of annihilation which it intended for us… It now perishes according to its own precept of 'an eye for an eye and a tooth for a tooth'!"

In 1939, in a speech to the Reichstag, Hitler had said:

"If international finance Jewry in and outside Europe should succeed in thrusting the nations once again into a world war, then the result will not be the Bolshevisation of the earth and with it the victory of Jewry, but the destruction of the Jewish race in Europe."

The view of most historians is that the decision to proceed with the extermination of the Jews was taken at some point in late 1941, and Goebbels' comments make it clear that he knew in general terms, if not in detail, what was planned.

The decision in principle to deport the German and Austrian Jews to unspecified destinations "in the east" was made in

September. Goebbels immediately pressed for the Berlin Jews to be deported first. He travelled to Hitler's headquarters on the eastern front, meeting both Hitler and Reinhard Heydrich to lobby for his demands. He got the assurances he wanted: "The Führer is of the opinion," he wrote, "that the Jews eventually have to be removed from the whole of Germany. The first cities to be made Jew-free are Berlin, Vienna and Prague. Berlin is first in the queue, and I have the hope that we'll succeed in the course of this year."

Deportations of Berlin Jews to the Łódź ghetto began in October, but transport and other difficulties made the process much slower than Goebbels desired. His November article in *Das Reich* was part of his campaign to have the pace of deportation accelerated.

In December, he was present when Hitler addressed a meeting of *Gauleiter*s and other senior Nazis, discussing among other things the "Jewish question." He wrote in his diary afterward:

With regard to the Jewish Question, the Führer is determined to make a clean sweep of it. He prophesied that, if they brought

(Left) A Hitler Youth recruiting poster emphasises the close link with the Furher. (Right) A propaganda magazine from 1939 'On the Westfront.'

about another world war, they would experience their annihilation. That was no empty talk. The world war is here (this was the week Germany declared war on the United States). The annihilation of Jewry must be the necessary consequence. The question is to be viewed without any sentimentality. We're not there to have sympathy with the Jews, but only sympathy with our own German people. If the German people has again now sacrificed around 160,000 dead in the eastern campaign, the originators of this bloody conflict will have to pay for it with their lives.

During 1942, Goebbels continued to press for the "final solution to the Jewish question" to be carried forward as quickly as possible now that Germany had occupied a huge swathe of Soviet territory into which all the Jews of German-controlled Europe could be deported. There they could be worked into extinction in accordance with the plan agreed on at the Wannsee Conference convened by Heydrich in January. It was a constant annoyance to Goebbels that, at a time when Germany was fighting for its life on the eastern front, there were still 40,000 Jews in Berlin. They should be "carted off to Russia," he wrote in his diary. "It would be best to kill them altogether." Although the Propaganda Ministry was not invited to the Wannsee Conference, Goebbels knew by March what had been decided there. He wrote:

The Jews are now being deported to the east. A fairly barbaric procedure, not to be described in any greater detail, is being used here, and not much more remains of the Jews themselves. In general, it can probably be established that 60 percent of them must be liquidated, while only 40 percent can be put to work… A judgment is being carried out on the Jews which is barbaric, but fully deserved.

PLENIPOTENTIARY FOR TOTAL WAR

Goebbels struggled in 1943 and 1944 to rally the German people behind a regime that faced increasingly obvious military defeat.

The German people's faith in Hitler was shaken by the disaster at Stalingrad, and never fully recovered. During 1943, as the Soviet armies advanced towards the borders of the Reich, the western Allies developed the ability to launch devastating air raids on most German cities, including Berlin. At the same time, there were increasingly critical shortages of food, raw materials, fuel and housing. Goebbels and Speer were among the few Nazi leaders who were under no illusions about Germany's dire situation. Their solution was to seize control of the home front from the indecisive Hitler and the incompetent Göring. This was the agenda of Goebbels's "total war" speech of February 1943. But they were thwarted by their inability to challenge Hitler, who could neither make decisions himself nor trust anyone else to do so.

After Stalingrad, Hitler increasingly withdrew from public view, almost never appearing in public and rarely even broadcasting. By July, Goebbels was lamenting that Hitler had cut himself off from the people – it was noted, for example, that he never visited the bomb-ravaged cities of the Ruhr. "One can't neglect the people too long," he wrote. "They are the heart of

The heroic German soldiery is the subject for this 1940 war art.

our war effort." Goebbels himself became the public voice of the Nazi regime, both in his regular broadcasts and his weekly editorials in *Das Reich*. As Joachim Fest notes, Goebbels seemed to take a grim pleasure in the destruction of Germany's cities by the Allied bombing offensive: "It was, as one of his colleagues confirmed, almost a happy day for him when famous buildings were destroyed, because at such time he put into his speeches that ecstatic hatred which aroused the fanaticism of the tiring workers and spurred them to fresh efforts."

In public, Goebbels remained confident of German victory: "We live at the most critical period in the history of the Occident," he wrote in *Das Reich* in February 1943. "Any weakening of the spiritual and military defensive strength of our continent in its struggle with eastern Bolshevism brings with it the danger of a rapidly nearing decline in its will to resist... Our soldiers in the East will do their part. They will stop the storm from the steppes, and ultimately break it. They fight under unimaginable conditions. But they are fighting a good fight. They are fighting not only for our own security, but also for Europe's future."

In private, he was discouraged by the failure of his and Speer's campaign to gain control of the home front. In 1944 he made a now infamous list with "irreplaceable artists" called the *Gottbegnadeten* list with people such as Arno Breker, Richard Strauss and Johannes Heesters.

Goebbels remained preoccupied with the annihilation of the Jews, which was now reaching its climax in the extermination camps of eastern Poland. As in 1942, he was more outspoken about what was happening than Himmler would have liked: "Our state's security requires that we take whatever measures seem necessary to protect the German community from (the Jewish) threat," he wrote in May. "That leads to some difficult decisions, but they are unavoidable if we are to deal with the threat... None of the Führer's prophetic words has come so inevitably true as his prediction that if Jewry succeeded in provoking a second world war, the result would be not the destruction of the Aryan race, but rather the wiping out of the Jewish race. This process is of vast importance."

Following the Allied invasion of Italy and the fall of Benito Mussolini in September, he and Joachim von Ribbentrop raised with Hitler the possibility of secretly approaching Joseph Stalin and negotiating a separate peace behind the backs of the western Allies. Hitler, surprisingly, did not reject the idea of a separate peace with either side, but he told Goebbels that he should not negotiate from a position of weakness. A great German victory must occur before any negotiations should be undertaken, he reasoned. The German defeat at Kursk in July had, however, ended any possibility of this.

As Germany's military and economic situation grew steadily worse during 1944, Goebbels renewed his push, in alliance with Speer, to wrest control of the home front away from Göring. In July, following the Allied landings in France and the huge Soviet advances in Belarus, Hitler finally agreed to grant both of them increased powers. Speer took control of all economic and production matters away from Göring, and Goebbels took the title

9 March 1945: Goebbels awards a 16 year old Hitler Youth, Willi Hübner, the Iron Cross for his actions in the ongoing Battle for Berlin.

Reich Plenipotentiary for "Total War" (*Reichsbevollmächtigter für den totalen Kriegseinsatz an der Heimatfront*). At the same time, Himmler took over the Interior Ministry.

This trio – Goebbels, Himmler and Speer – became the real centre of German government in the last year of the war, although Bormann used his privileged access to Hitler to thwart them when he could. In this Bormann was very successful, as the party *Gauleiter*s gained more and more powers, becoming Reich Defense Commissars (*Reichsverteidigungskommissare*) in their respective districts and overseeing all civilian administration. The fact that Himmler was Interior Minister only increased the power of Bormann, as the *Gauleiter*s feared that Himmler, who was General Plenipotentiary for the Administration of the Reich, would curb their power and set up his higher SS and police leaders as their replacement.

Goebbels saw Himmler as a potential ally against Bormann and in 1944 is supposed to have voiced the opinion that if the *Reichsführer* SS was granted control over the Wehrmacht and he, Goebbels, granted control over the domestic politics, the war would soon be ended in a victorious manner. However, the inability of Himmler to persuade Hitler to cease his support of Bormann, the defection of SS generals such as *Obergruppenführer* Ernst Kaltenbrunner, the Chief of the *Reichssicherheitshauptamt* and his powerful subordinate *Gruppenführer* Heinrich Müller, the head of the Gestapo, to Bormann, soon persuaded Goebbels to align himself with the Secretary to the Führer at the end of 1944, thus accepting his subordinate position.

When elements of the army leadership tried to assassinate Hitler in the July 20 plot shortly thereafter, it was this trio that rallied the resistance to the plotters. It was Goebbels, besieged in his Berlin flat with Speer and secretary Wilfred von Oven beside him but with his phone lines intact, who brought Otto Ernst Remer, the wavering commander of the Berlin garrison, to the phone to speak to Hitler in East Prussia, thus demonstrating that the Führer was alive and that the garrison should oppose the attempted coup.

Goebbels promised Hitler that he could raise a million new soldiers by means of a reorganisation of the Army, transferring personnel from the Navy and *Luftwaffe*, and purging the bloated Reich Ministries, which satraps like Göring had hitherto protected. As it turned out, the inertia of the state bureaucracy was too great even for the energetic Goebbels to overcome. Bormann and his puppet Lammers, keen to retain their control over the Party and State administrations respectively, placed endless obstacles in Goebbels's way. Another problem was that although Speer and Goebbels were allies, their agendas in fact conflicted: Speer wanted absolute priority in the allocation of labour to be given to arms production, while Goebbels sought to press every able-bodied male into the army. Speer, allied with Fritz Sauckel, the General Plenipotentiary for the Employment of Labour from 1942, generally won these battles.

The iron will of the German worker signals death to the Marxist menace.

By July 1944, it was in any case too late for Goebbels and Speer's internal coup to make any real difference to the outcome of the war. The combined economic and military power of the western Allies and the Soviet Union, now fully mobilized, was simply too great for Germany to overcome. A crucial economic indicator, the ratio of steel output, was running at 4.5:1 against Germany. The final blow was the loss of the Romanian oil fields as the Soviet Army advanced through the Balkans in September. This, combined with the U.S. air campaign against Germany's synthetic oil production, finally broke the back of the German economy and thus its capacity for further resistance. By this time, the best Goebbels could do to reassure the German people that victory was still possible was to make vague promises that "miracle weapons" such as the Me 262 jet airplane, the Type XXI U-boat, and the V-2 rocket could somehow retrieve the military situation.

DEFEAT

In the last months of the war, Goebbels' speeches and articles took on an increasingly apocalyptic tone:

"Rarely in history has a brave people struggling for its life faced such terrible tests as the German people have in this war," he wrote towards the end. *"The misery that results for us all, the never ending chain of sorrows, fears, and spiritual torture does not need to be described in detail. We are bearing a heavy fate because we are fighting for a good cause, and are called to bravely endure the battle to achieve greatness."*

By the beginning of 1945, with the Soviets on the Oder and the Western Allies preparing to cross the Rhine, Goebbels could no longer disguise the fact that defeat was inevitable. He knew what that would mean for himself: "For us," he had written in 1943, "we have burnt our bridges. We cannot go back, but neither do we want to go back. We are forced to extremes and therefore resolved to proceed to extremes." In his diaries, he expressed the belief that German diplomacy should find a way to exploit the emerging tensions between Stalin and the West, but he proclaimed foreign minister Joachim von Ribbentrop, whom Hitler would not abandon, incapable of such a feat.

When other Nazi leaders urged Hitler to leave Berlin and establish a new centre of resistance in the National Redoubt in Bavaria, Goebbels opposed this, arguing for a last stand in the ruins of the Reich capital.

By this time, Goebbels had gained the position he had wanted so long – at the side of Hitler, albeit only because of his subservience to Bormann, who was the Führer's de facto deputy. Göring was utterly discredited, though Hitler refused to dismiss him until 25 April. Himmler, whose appointment as commander of Army Group Vistula had led to disaster on the Oder, was also in disgrace, and Hitler rightly suspected that he was secretly trying to negotiate with the western Allies. Only Goebbels and Bormann remained totally loyal to Hitler. Goebbels knew how to play on

(Left) Wehrmacht - Heer recruiting poster. (Right) A recruiting poster seeking Norwegian volounteers for the Noregian Ski battalion of the SS.

Hitler's fantasies, encouraging him to see the hand of providence in the death of United States President Franklin D. Roosevelt on 12 April. On 22 April, largely as a result of Goebbels' influence, Hitler announced that he would not leave Berlin, but would stay and fight, and if necessary die, in defence of the capital.

On 23 April, Goebbels made the following proclamation to the people of Berlin:

"I call on you to fight for your city. Fight with everything you have got, for the sake of your wives and your children, your mothers and your parents. Your arms are defending everything we have ever held dear, and all the generations that will come after us. Be proud and courageous! Be inventive and cunning! Your Gauleiter is amongst you. He and his colleagues will remain in your midst. His wife and children are here as well. He, who once captured the city with 200 men, will now use every means to galvanize the defence of the capital. The battle for Berlin must become the signal for the whole nation to rise up in battle…"

Unlike many other leading Nazis at this juncture, Goebbels proved to have strong convictions, moving himself and his family into the *Vorbunker*, that was connected to the lower *Führerbunker* under the Reich Chancellery gardens in central Berlin. He told Vice-Admiral Hans-Erich Voss that he would not entertain the idea of either surrender or escape: "I was the Reich Minister of Propaganda and led the fiercest activity against the Soviet Union, for which they would never pardon me," Voss quoted him as saying. "He couldn't escape also because he was Berlin's Defence Commissioner and he considered it would be disgraceful for him to abandon his post," Voss added.

After midnight on 29 April, with the Soviets advancing ever closer to the bunker complex, Hitler dictated his last will and testament. Goebbels was one of four witnesses. In the mid-afternoon of 30 April, Hitler shot himself. Of Hitler's death, Goebbels commented: "The heart of Germany has ceased to beat. The Führer is dead."

In his last will and testament, Hitler named no successor as Führer or leader of the Nazi Party. Instead, Hitler appointed Goebbels Reich Chancellor; Grand Admiral Karl Dönitz, who was at Flensburg near the Danish border, Reich President; and Martin Bormann, Hitler's long-time chief of staff, Party Minister. Goebbels knew that this was an empty title. Even if he was willing and able to escape Berlin and reach the north, it was unlikely that Dönitz, whose only concern was to negotiate a settlement with the western Allies that would save Germany from Soviet occupation, would want such a notorious figure as Goebbels heading his government.

As it was, Goebbels had no intention of trying to escape. Voss later recounted: "When Goebbels learned that Hitler had committed suicide, he was very depressed and said: 'It is a great pity that such a man is not with us any longer. But there is nothing

(Left) The iconic image of the Waffen SS came from this recruiting poster. (Right) A Dutch recruitment poster calls for volunteers to join the Waffen SS. Despite the strength of the image the numbers joining were inconsequential.

to be done. For us, everything is lost now and the only way left for us is the one which Hitler chose. I shall follow his example'."

On 1 May, Goebbels completed his sole official act as Chancellor of Germany (*Reichskanzler*). He dictated a letter and ordered German General Hans Krebs, under a white flag, to meet with General Vasily Chuikov and to deliver his letter. Chuikov, as commander of the Soviet 8th Guards Army, commanded the Soviet forces in central Berlin. Goebbels' letter informed Chuikov of Hitler's death and requested a ceasefire, hinting that the establishment of a National Socialist government hostile to Western plutocracy would be beneficial to the Soviet Union, as the betrayal of Himmler and Göring indicated that otherwise anti-Soviet National Socialist elements might align themselves with the West. When this was rejected, Goebbels decided that further efforts were futile. Shortly afterward he dictated a postscript to Hitler's testament:

The Führer has given orders for me, in case of a breakdown of defence of the Capital of the Reich, to leave Berlin and to participate as a leading member in a government appointed by him. For the first time in my life, I must categorically refuse to obey a command of the Führer. My wife and my children agree with this refusal. In any other case, I would feel myself... a dishonorable renegade and vile scoundrel for my entire further life, who would lose the esteem of himself along with the esteem of his people, both of which would have to form the requirement for further duty of my person in designing the future of the German Nation and the German Reich.

- C H A P T E R 6 -
NAZI PROPAGANDA

IN POWER (1933–39)

BEFORE WORLD War II, Nazi propaganda strategy, officially promulgated by the Ministry of Public Enlightenment and Propaganda, stressed several themes. Their goals were to establish external enemies (countries that allegedly inflicted the Treaty of Versailles on Germany) and internal enemies, such as Jews, Romani, homosexuals, and Bolsheviks. Hitler and Nazi propagandists played on the anti-Semitism and resentment present in Germany. The Jews were blamed for things such as robbing the German people of their hard work while themselves avoiding physical labour. *Der Stürmer*, a Nazi propaganda newspaper, told Germans that Jews kidnapped small children before Passover because "Jews need the blood of a Christian child, maybe, to mix in with their Matzah." Posters, films, cartoons, and fliers were seen throughout Germany which attacked the Jewish community, such as the 1940 film *The Eternal Jew*.

Reaching out to ethnic Germans in other countries such as Czechoslovakia, France, Poland, the Soviet Union and the Baltic states was another aim of Nazi party propaganda. In *Mein Kampf*, Hitler makes a direct remark to those outside of Germany. He states that pain and misery is forced upon ethnic Germans outside of Germany, and that they dream of common fatherland. He finished by stating they needed to fight for one's nationality. Throughout *Mein Kampf*, he pushed Germans worldwide to make the struggle for political power and independence their main focus.

Nazi propaganda efforts then focused on creating external enemies. Propagandists strengthened the negative attitude of Germany towards the Treaty of Versailles by territorial claims and ethnocentrism. When the Treaty was signed in 1919 non-

A 1937 anti-Bolshevik Nazi propaganda poster. The translated caption: "Bolshevism without a mask - large anti-Bolshevik exhibition of the NSDAP Gauleitung Berlin from November 6, 1937 to December 19, 1937 in the Reichstag building".

propagandists newspapers headlines across the nation spoke German's feelings, such as "UNACCEPTABLE" which appeared on the front page of the Frankfurter Zeitung in 1919. The Berliner Tageblatt, also in 1919, predicted "Should we accept the conditions, a military furore for revenge will sound in Germany within a few years, a militant nationalism will engulf all." Hitler, knowing his nation's disgust with the Treaty, used it as leverage to influence his audience. He would repeatedly refer back to the terms of the Treaty as a direct attack on Germany and its people. In one speech delivered on January 30, 1937 he directly states that he is withdrawing the German signature from the document to protest the outrageous proportions of the terms. He claims the Treaty makes Germany out to be inferior and "less" of a country than others only because blame for the war is placed on it. The success of Nazi propagandists and Hitler won the Nazi party control of Germany and eventually led to World War II.

For months prior to the beginning of World War II in 1939, German newspapers and leaders had carried out a national and international propaganda campaign accusing Polish authorities of organizing or tolerating violent ethnic cleansing of ethnic Germans living in Poland. On 22 August, Adolf Hitler told his generals:

"I will provide a propagandistic casus belli. Its credibility doesn't matter. The victor will not be asked whether he told the truth."

The main part of this propaganda campaign was the false flag project, Operation Himmler, which was designed to create the appearance of Polish aggression against Germany, which was subsequently used to justify the invasion of Poland.

AT WAR (1939–45)

Until the conclusion of the Battle of Stalingrad on February 4, 1943, German propaganda emphasized the prowess of German arms and the humanity German soldiers had shown to the peoples of occupied territories. Pilots of the Allied bombing fleets were depicted as cowardly murderers, and Americans in particular as gangsters in the style of Al Capone. At the same time, German propaganda sought to alienate Americans and British from each other, and both these Western nations from the Soviets. One of the primary sources for propaganda was the *Wehrmachtbericht*, a daily radio broadcast that described the military situation on all fronts. Nazi victories lent themselves easily to propaganda broadcasts and were at this point difficult to mishandle. Satires on the defeated, accounts of attacks, and praise for the fallen all were useful for Nazis. Still, failures were not easily handled even at this stage; when the Ark Royal proved to have survived an attack that German propaganda had hyped, considerable embarrassment resulted.

After Stalingrad, the main theme changed to Germany as the sole defender of what they called "Western European culture" against the "Bolshevist hordes". The introduction of the V-1 and V-2 "vengeance weapons" was emphasized to convince Britons of the hopelessness of defeating Germany.

Problems in propaganda arose easily in this stage; expectations of success were raised too high and too quickly, which required explanation if they were not fulfilled, and blunted the effects of success, and the hushing of blunders and failures caused mistrust. The increasing hardship of the war for the German people also called forth more propaganda that the war had been forced on the German people by the refusal of foreign powers to accept their strength and independence. Goebbels called for propaganda to toughen up the German people and not make victory look easy.

On June 23, 1944, the Nazis permitted the Red Cross to visit concentration camp Theresienstadt to dispel rumours about the Final Solution, which was intended to kill every Jew. In reality, Theresienstadt was a transit camp for Jews en route to extermination camps, but in a sophisticated propaganda effort, fake shops and cafés were erected to imply that the Jews lived in relative comfort. The guests enjoyed the performance of a children's opera, Brundibar, written by inmate Hans Krása. The hoax was so successful for the Nazis that they went on to make a propaganda film (*Theresienstadt*) at Theresienstadt. Shooting of the film began on February 26, 1944. Directed by Kurt Gerron, it was meant to show how well the Jews lived under the "benevolent" protection of the Third Reich. After the shooting, most of the cast, and even the filmmaker himself, were deported to the concentration camp of Auschwitz where they were killed.

Goebbels committed suicide on May 1, 1945, shortly after Hitler had killed himself. Hans Fritzsche, who had been head of the Radio Chamber, was tried and acquitted by the Nuremberg war crimes tribunal.

MEDIA IN THE THIRD REICH

NEWSPAPERS

The *Völkischer Beobachter* ("People's Observer") was the official daily newspaper of the NSDAP since December 1920. It disseminated Nazi ideology in the form of brief hyperboles directed against the weakness of parliamentarism, the evils of Jewry and Bolshevism, the national humiliation of the Versailles Treaty and other such topics. It was joined in 1926 by *Der Angriff* ("The Attack"), a weekly and later daily paper founded by Joseph Goebbels. It was mainly dedicated to attacks against political opponents and Jews – one of its most striking features were vehemently antisemitic cartoons by Hans Schweitzer – but also engaged in the glorification of Nazi heroes such as Horst Wessel. The *Illustrierter Beobachter* was their weekly illustrated paper.

Other Nazi publications included

- *Das Reich*, a more moderate and highbrow publication aimed at intellectuals and foreigners;
- *Der Stürmer*, the most virulently antisemitic of all; and

- *Das Schwarze Korps*, an SS publication, aiming at a more intellectual tone.

After Hitler's rise to power in 1933, all of the regular press came under complete Nazi editorial control through the policy of *Gleichschaltung*, and short-lived propaganda newspapers were also established in the conquered territories during World War II.

NEWSPAPERS IN OCCUPIED COUNTRIES

In Ukraine, after Nazis cracked down on the papers, most printed only articles from German agencies, producing the odd effect of more anti-American and anti-British articles than anti-Communist ones. They also printed articles about antecedents of German rule over Ukraine, such as Catherine the Great and the Goths.

SPEAKERS

The Nazi party relied heavily on speakers to make its propaganda presentations, most heavily before they came to power, but also afterwards. Hitler, in Mein Kampf, recounted that he had realized that it was not written matter but the spoken word that brought about changes, as people would not read things that disagreed, but would linger to hear a speaker. Furthermore, speakers, having their audiences before them, could see their reactions and adjust accordingly, to persuade. His own oratory was a major factor in his rise, and he despised those who came to read pre-written speeches.

Such speakers were particularly important when it was not wanted that the information put across not reach foreigners, who could access the mass media. Schools were instituted to substitute for the political conflict that had formed the old speakers. In 1939, Walter Tiessler, speaking of his own experience as an early speaker, urged that they continue.

Sturmabteilung speakers were used, though their reliance on instinct sometimes offended well-educated audiences, but their blunt and folksy manner often had their own appeal.

The ministry would provide such speakers with information, such as how to spin the problems on the eastern front, or how to discuss the cuts in food rations. The party propaganda headquarters, sent the *Redner-Schnellinformation* (Speakers' Express Information) out with guidelines for immediate campaigns, such as anti-Semitic campaigns and what information to present.

Specific groups were targeted with such speakers. Speakers, for instance, were created specifically for Hitler Youth. These would, among other things, lecture Hitler Youth and the BDM on the need to produce more children.

POSTERS

Poster art was a mainstay of the Nazi propaganda effort, aimed both at Germany itself and occupied territories. It had several

(Left) Enemies lurk in the shadows, part of the Pst! series warning the German civilian population to be on guard at all times against spies and saboteurs. (Right) Another in the Pst! series of warning posters.

advantages. The visual effect, being striking, would reach the viewer easily. Posters were also, unlike other forms of propaganda, difficult to avoid.

Imagery frequently drew on heroic realism. Nazi youth and the SS were depicted monumentally, with lighting posed to produce grandeur. Hans Schweitzer, under the pen name *"Mjölnir"* produced many Nazi posters.

Posters were also used in schools, depicting, for instance, an institution for the feeble-minded on one hand and houses on the other, to inform the students that the annual cost of this institution would build 17 homes for healthy families.

FILMS

The Nazis produced many films to promote their views. Themes included the virtues of the Nordic or Aryan type, German military and industrial strength, and the evils of the Nazi enemies. On March

(Left) The danger of spies posing in mundane roles such as waiters is evoked in this Pst! poster. (Right) The idea that the enemy has ears everywhere is hammered home by this highly effective poster.

13, 1933, The Third Reich established a Ministry of Propaganda, appointing Joseph Goebbels as its Minister. On September 22, 1933, a Department of Film was incorporated into the Chamber of Culture. The department controlled the licensing of every film prior to its production. Sometimes, the government would select the actors for a film, financing the production partially or totally, and would grant tax breaks to the producers. Awards for "valuable" films would decrease taxes, thus encouraging self-censorship among movie makers.

Under Goebbels and Hitler, the German film industry became entirely nationalised. The National Socialist Propaganda Directorate, which Goebbels oversaw, had at its disposal nearly all film agencies in Germany by 1936. Occasionally, certain directors such as Wolfgang Liebeneiner were able to bypass Goebbels by providing him with a different version of the film than would be released. Such films include those directed by Helmut Käutner: Romanze in Moll (Romance in a Minor Key, 1943), Große Freiheit Nr. 7 (The Great Freedom, No. 7, 1944), and Unter den Brücken (Under the Bridges, 1945).

Schools were also provided with motion pictures projectors because film was regarded as particularly appropriate for propagandizing children. Films specifically created for schools were termed "military education."

Newsreels were explicitly intended to not be the truth, but to portray such of the truth as was in the interest of Germany to spread.

Triumph des Willens (Triumph of the Will, 1934) by film-maker Leni Riefenstahl chronicles the Nazi Party Congress in Nuremberg. It features footage of uniformed party members (though relatively few German soldiers), who are marching and drilling to classical melodies. The film contains excerpts from speeches given by various Nazi leaders at the Congress, including speeches by Adolf Hitler. Frank Capra used scenes from the film, which he described partially as "the ominous prelude of Hitler's holocaust of hate" in many parts of the U.S. government's Why We Fight anti-Axis seven film series, to demonstrate what the personnel of the American military would be facing in World War II, and why the Axis had to be defeated.

Der ewige Jude (The Eternal Jew, 1940) was directed by Fritz Hippler at the insistence of Goebbels, though the writing is credited to Eberhard Taubert. The movie is done in the style of a documentary, the central thesis being the immutable racial personality traits that characterize the Jew as a wandering cultural parasite. Throughout the film, these traits are contrasted to the Nazi state ideal: while Aryan men find satisfaction in physical labour and the creation of value, Jews only find pleasure in money and a hedonist lifestyle.

BOOKS

The Nazis and sympathizers published many books. Most of the beliefs that would become associated with the Nazis, such as German nationalism, eugenics and anti-Semitism had been in circulation since the 19th century, and the Nazis seized on this body of existing work in their own publications.

The most notable is Adolf Hitler's *Mein Kampf* detailing his beliefs. The book outlines major ideas that would later culminate in World War II. It is heavily influenced by Gustave Le Bon's 1895 The Crowd: A Study of the Popular Mind, which theorized propaganda as a way to control the seemingly irrational behaviour of crowds. Particularly prominent is the violent anti-Semitism of Hitler and his associates, drawing, among other sources, on the fabricated "Protocols of the Elders of Zion". For example, Hitler claimed that the international language Esperanto was part of a Jewish plot and makes arguments toward the old German nationalist ideas of "*Drang nach Osten*" and the necessity to gain *Lebensraum* ("living space") eastwards (especially in Russia).

Other books such as *Rassenkunde des deutschen Volkes*

(Ethnology of German People) by Hans F. K. Günther and *Rasse und Seele* (Race and Soul) by Dr. Ludwig Ferdinand Clauss attempt to identify and classify the differences between the German, Nordic or Aryan type and other supposedly inferior peoples. These books were used as texts in German schools during the Nazi era.

The pre-existing and popular genre of Schollen-roman, or novel of the soil, also known as blood and soil novels, was given a boost by the acceptability of its themes to the Nazis and developed a mysticism of unity.

The immensely popular "Red Indian" stories by Karl May were permitted despite the heroic treatment of the hero Winnetou and "coloured" races; instead, the argument was made that the stories demonstrated the fall of the Red Indians was caused by a lack of racial consciousness, to encourage it in the Germans. Other fictional works were also adapted; Heidi was stripped of its Christian elements, and Robinson Crusoe's relationship to Friday was made a master-slave one.

(Left) 'Just as we fight... you fight with us for victory!'
(Right) A recruiting poster designed to elicit volunteers for the infantry 'The Queen of the Battlefield.'

TEXT BOOKS

"Geopolitical atlases" emphasized Nazi schemes, demonstrating the "encirclement" of Germany, depicting how the prolific Slav nations would cause the German people to be overrun, and (in contrast) showing the relative population density of Germany was much higher than that of the Eastern regions (where they would seek *Lebensraum*). Geography text books stated how crowded Germany had become. Other charts would show the cost of disabled children as opposed to healthy ones, or show how two-child families threatened the birthrate.

Math books discussed military applications and used military word problems, physics and chemistry concentrated on military applications, and grammar classes were devoted to propaganda sentences. Other textbooks dealt with the history of the Nazi Party. Elementary school reading text included large amounts of propaganda.

(Left) A Luftwaffe recruiting poster. (Right) The Jew is demonised as the root cause of the war and the prolonger of war through profiteering.

Maps showing the racial composition of Europe were banned from the classroom after many efforts that did not define the territory widely enough for party officials.

Even fairy tales were put to use, with Cinderella being presented as a tale of how the prince's racial instincts lead him to reject the stepmother's alien blood for the racially pure maiden. Nordic sagas were likewise presented as the illustration of *Führerprinzip*, which was developed with such heroes as Frederick the Great and Bismark.

Literature was to be chosen within the "German spirit" rather than a fixed list of forbidden and required, which made the teachers all the more cautious although Jewish authors were impossible for classrooms. While only William Shakespeare's Macbeth and The Merchant of Venice were actually recommended, none of the plays were actually forbidden, even Hamlet, denounced for "flabbiness of soul."

Biology texts, however, were put the most use in presenting eugenic principles and racial theories; this included explanations of the Nuremberg Laws, which were claimed to allow the German and Jewish peoples to co-exist without the danger of mixing. Science was to be presented as the most natural area for introducing the "Jewish Question", once teachers took care to point out that in nature, animals associated with those of their own species.

Teachers' guidelines on racial instruction presented both the handicapped and Jews as dangers. Despite their many photographs glamorizing the "Nordic" type, the texts also claimed that visual inspection was insufficient, and genealogical analysis was required to determine their types, and report any hereditary problems.

BOOKS FOR OCCUPIED COUNTRIES

In occupied France, the German Institute encouraged translation of German works, although chiefly German nationalists, not ardent

Nazis, and produced a massive increase in the sale of translated works. The only books from English to be sold were English classics, and books with Jewish authors or Jewish subject matter (such as biographies) were banned, except for some scientific works. Control of the paper supply allowed Germans the easy ability to pressure publishers about books.

COMICS

The Nazi-controlled government in German-occupied France produced the Vica comic book series during World War II as a propaganda tool against the Allied forces. The Vica series, authored by Vincent Krassousky, represented Nazi influence and perspective in French society, and included such titles as *Vica contre le service secret anglais*, and *Vica défie l'Oncle Sam*.

MAGAZINES

In and after 1939, the *Zeitschriften-Dienst* was sent to magazines to provide guidelines on what to write for appropriate topics.

Nazi publications also carried various forms of propaganda.

Neues Volk, the monthly publication of the Office of Racial Policy, carried racial propaganda. While chiefly aimed at fomenting ethnic pride through ideal Aryan types, it also included articles aimed at Jews and "defectives."

The *NS-Frauen-Warte*, aimed at women, included such topics as the role of women in the Nazi state. Despite its propaganda elements, it was predominately a woman's magazine. It defended anti-intellectualism, urged women to have children, even in wartime, put forth what the Nazis had done for women, discusses bridal schools, urged women to greater efforts in total war.

Der Pimpf was aimed at boys and contained both adventure and propaganda.

Das deutsche Mädel, in contrast, recommended for girls hiking, tending the wounded, and preparing for care for children. It lay far more emphasis than *NS-Frauen-Warte* on the strong and active German woman.

SIGNAL

Signal was a propaganda magazine published by the Wehrmacht during World War II. It was distributed throughout occupied Europe and neutral countries. "Signal" was published from April 1940 to March 1945, and had the highest sales of any magazine published in Europe during the period 1940 to 1945 - circulation peaked at two and one half million in 1943. At various times, it was published in at least twenty languages. There was an English edition distributed in the British Channel Islands of Guernsey, Jersey, Alderney, and Sark - these islands were occupied by the Wehrmacht during World War II.

(Left) A 1943 poster commemorating 10 years of Nazi rule proclaiming 'One struggle... one victory!'
(Right) Recruiting poster for the Hermann Goring Division.

The promoter of the magazine was the chief of the Wehrmacht propaganda office, Colonel Hasso von Wedel. Its annual budget was 10 million Reichmarks, roughly $2.5 million at the pre-war exchange rate.

The image that Signal hoped to create was that of Nazi Germany and its New Order as the great benefactor of European peoples and of Western civilization in general. Germany and its allies were depicted as the humane liberators of the occupied nations. Some articles displayed colour photographs of dramatic battle scenes. The magazine contained little anti-Semitic propaganda, and the Jews were hardly mentioned.

RADIO

The radio was an important tool in Nazi propaganda and it has been argued that it was the Nazis who pioneered the use of what was still a relatively new technology as a tool of genocide.

INTERNAL BROADCASTS

Certainly the Nazis recognised the importance of radio in disseminating their message and to that end Goebbels approved a scheme whereby millions of cheap radio sets (the *Volksempfänger*) were subsidised by the government. Goebbels claimed the radio was the "eighth great power", and he, along with the Nazi party, recognized the power of the radio in the propaganda machine of Nazi Germany. In that "Radio as the Eighth Great Power" speech, Goebbels proclaimed:

"It would not have been possible for us to take power or to use it in the ways we have without the radio....It is no exaggeration to say that the German revolution, at least in the form it took, would have been impossible without the airplane and the radio... (Radio) reached the entire nation, regardless of class, standing, or religion. That was primarily the result of the tight centralization,

the strong reporting, and the up-to-date nature of the German radio."

By the start of the Second World War over 70% of German households had one of these radios, which were deliberately limited in range in order to prevent loyal citizens from considering other viewpoints in foreign broadcasts. Radio broadcasts were also played over loudspeakers in public places and workplaces.

In private homes, however, people could easily turn off the radio when bored and did so once the novelty of hearing the voice from a box wore off; this caused the Nazis to introduce many non-propaganda elements, such as music, advice and tips, serials and other entertainment. This was accelerated in the war to prevent people from tuning in enemy propaganda broadcasts; though Goebbels claimed in his *Das Reich* article that it was to make the radio a good companion to the people, he admitted the truth in his diary.

EXTERNAL BROADCASTS

As well as domestic broadcasts, the Nazi regime also used radio to deliver its message to both occupied territories and enemy states. One of the main targets was the United Kingdom to where William Joyce broadcast regularly, gaining the nickname 'Lord Haw-Haw' in the process. Joyce first appeared on German radio on 6 September 1939 reading the news in English but soon became noted for his often mischievous propaganda broadcasts. Joyce was executed in 1946 for treason. Although the most notorious, and most regularly heard, of the UK propagandists, Joyce was not the only broadcaster, with others such as Norman Baillie-Stewart, Jersey-born teacher Pearl Vardon, British Union of Fascists members Leonard Banning and Susan Hilton, Barry Payne Jones of the Link and Alexander Fraser Grant, whose show was aimed specifically at Scotland, also broadcasting through the 'New British Broadcasting Service'.

Broadcasts were also made to the United States, notably through Robert Henry Best and 'Axis Sally' Mildred Gillars. Best, a freelance journalist based in Vienna, was initially arrested following the German declaration of war on the US but before long he became a feature on propaganda radio, attacking the influence of the Jews in the US and the leadership of Franklin Delano Roosevelt. He would later be sentenced to life imprisonment for treason. Gilders, a teacher in Germany, mostly broadcast on similar themes as well as peppering her speech with allegations of infidelity against the wives of servicemen. Her most notorious broadcast was the 'Vision of Invasion' radio play, broadcast immediately prior to D-Day, from the perspective of an American mother who dreamed that her soldier son died violently in Normandy.

France also received broadcasts from Radio-Stuttgart, where Paul Ferdonnet, an anti-Semitic journalist, was the main voice during the Phoney War. Following the occupation Radio Paris and Radio Vichy became the main organs of propaganda, with leading far right figures such as Jacques Doriot, Philippe Henriot and Jean Hérold-Paquis regularly speaking in support of the Nazis. Others who broadcast included Gerald Hewitt, a British citizen who lived most of his life in Paris and had been associated with *Action Française*. The use of domestic broadcasters intended to galvanise support for occupation was also used in Belgium, where Ward Hermans regularly spoke in support of the Nazis from his base in Bremen, and the Italian Social Republic, to where Giovanni Preziosi broadcast a vehemently anti-Semitic show from his base in Munich. Pro-Nazi broadcasts were even heard in North Africa, where Mohammad Amin al-Husayni helped to ensure the spread of Nazi ideas in the Arabic language.

THEMES IN NAZI PROPAGANDA

Nazi propaganda promoted Nazi ideology by demonizing the enemies of the Nazi Party, especially Jews and communists, but also capitalists and intellectuals. It promoted the values asserted by the Nazis, including heroic death, *Führerprinzip* (leader principle), *Volksgemeinschaft* (people's community), *Blut und Boden* (blood and soil) and pride in the German race. Propaganda was also used to maintain the cult of personality around Nazi leader Adolf Hitler, and to promote campaigns for eugenics and the annexation of German-speaking areas. After the outbreak of World War II, Nazi propaganda vilified Germany's enemies, notably the United Kingdom, the Soviet Union and the United States, and exhorted the population to partake in total war.

HISTORIOGRAPHY

Nazi propaganda is a relatively recent topic of close study. Historians of all persuasions, including Eastern Bloc writers, agree about its remarkable effectiveness. Their assessment of its significance, however – whether it shaped or merely directed and exploited public opinion – is influenced by their approach to wider questions raised by the study of Nazi Germany, such as the question whether the Nazi state was a fully totalitarian dictatorship, as argued by Hannah Arendt, or whether it also depended on a certain societal consensus.

In addition to media archives, an important primary source for the study of the Nazi propaganda effort are the reports on civilian morale and public opinion that the *Sicherheitsdienst* and later the RMVP compiled from 1939 on. Another are the *Deutschland-Berichte*, reports gathered by underground agents of the Sopade that particularly dealt with German popular opinion.

- C H A P T E R   7 -
ART OF THE THIRD REICH

THE ART of the Third Reich, the officially approved art produced in Nazi Germany between 1933 and 1945, was characterized by a style of Romantic realism based on classical models. While banning modern styles as degenerate, the Nazis promoted paintings and sculptures that were narrowly traditional in manner and that exalted the "blood and soil" values of racial purity, militarism, and obedience. Other popular themes for Nazi art were the Volk at work in the fields, a return to the simple virtues of Heimat (love of homeland), the manly virtues of the National Socialist struggle, and the lauding of the female activities of child bearing and raising (Kinder, Küche, Kirche).

Similarly, music was expected to be tonal and free of jazz influence; films and plays were censored. Nazi art bears a close similarity to the Soviet propaganda art style of Socialist Realism, and the term heroic realism has sometimes been used to describe both artistic styles.Among the well-known artists endorsed by the Nazis were the sculptors Josef Thorak and Arno Breker, and painters Werner Peiner, Adolf Wissel and Conrad Hommel.

HISTORICAL BACKGROUND

The early twentieth century was characterized by startling changes in artistic styles. In the visual arts, such innovations as cubism, Dada and surrealism, following hot on the heels of Symbolism, post-Impressionism and Fauvism, were not universally appreciated. The majority of people in Germany, as elsewhere, did not care for the new art which many resented as elitist, morally suspect and too often incomprehensible.

During recent years, Germany had become a major centre of avant-garde art. It was the birthplace of Expressionism in painting and sculpture, the atonal musical compositions of Arnold Schoenberg, and the jazz-influenced work of Paul Hindemith and Kurt Weill. Robert Wiene's *The Cabinet of Dr. Caligari and Fritz Lang's Metropolis* brought expressionism to cinema.

The Nazis viewed the culture of the Weimar period with disgust. Their response stemmed partly from conservative aesthetics and partly from their determination to use culture as propaganda. Upon becoming dictator in 1933, Adolf Hitler gave his personal artistic preference the force of law to a degree rarely known before. Only in Joseph Stalin's Soviet Union, where Socialist Realism had become the mandatory style, had a state shown such concern with regulation of the arts. In the case of Germany, the model was to be classical Greek and Roman art, seen by Hitler as an art whose exterior form embodied an inner racial ideal. It was, furthermore, to be comprehensible to the average man. This art was to be both heroic and romantic.

The reason for this, as historian Henry Grosshans indicates, is that Hitler "saw Greek and Roman art as uncontaminated by Jewish influences. Modern art was (seen as) an act of aesthetic violence by the Jews against the German spirit. Such was true to Hitler even though only Liebermann, Meidner, Freundlich, and Marc Chagall, among those who made significant contributions to the German modernist movement, were Jewish. But Hitler... took upon himself the responsibility of deciding who, in matters of culture, thought and acted like a Jew."

The supposedly "Jewish" nature of art that was indecipherable, distorted, or that represented "depraved" subject matter was explained through the concept of degeneracy, which held that distorted and corrupted art was a symptom of an inferior race. By propagating the theory of degeneracy, the Nazis combined their anti-Semitism with their drive to control the culture, thus consolidating public support for both campaigns.

Their efforts in this regard were unquestionably aided by a popular hostility to Modernism that predated their movement. The view that such art had reflected Germany's condition and moral bankruptcy was widespread, and many artists acted in a manner to overtly undermine or challenge popular values and morality.

DEGENERATE ART

The term *Entartung* (or "degeneracy") had gained popularity in Germany by the late 19th century when the critic and author Max Nordau devised the theory presented in his 1892 book, *Entartung*. Nordau drew upon the writings of the criminologist Cesare Lombroso, whose *The Criminal Man*, published in 1876, attempted to prove that there were "born criminals" whose atavistic personality traits could be detected by scientifically measuring abnormal physical characteristics. Nordau developed from this premise a critique of modern art, explained as the work of those so corrupted and enfeebled by modern life that they have lost the self-control needed to produce coherent works. Explaining

'Stormtroops Advancing Under Gas', etching and aquatint by Otto Dix, 1924. Dix was among the artists condemned as entartet. The distorted bodies, reflecting the horror and despair of war, were at odds with the desire to glorify the martial vigor and confidence of the German people.

the painterliness of Impressionism as the sign of a diseased visual cortex, he decried modern degeneracy while praising traditional German culture. Despite the fact that Nordau was Jewish (as was Lombroso), his theory of artistic degeneracy would be seized upon by German National Socialists during the Weimar Republic as a rallying point for their anti-Semitic and racist demand for Aryan purity in art.

Belief in a Germanic spirit - defined as mystical, rural, moral, bearing ancient wisdom, noble in the face of a tragic destiny - existed long before the rise of the Nazis; Richard Wagner celebrated such ideas in his work. Beginning before World War I the well-known German architect and painter Paul Schultze-Naumburg's influential writings, which invoked racial theories in condemning modern art and architecture, supplied much of the basis for Adolf Hitler's belief that classical Greece and the Middle Ages were the true sources of Aryan art. Hitler's rise to power on January 31, 1933 was quickly followed by actions intended to cleanse the culture of degeneracy: book burnings were organized, artists and musicians were dismissed from teaching positions, artists were forbidden to utilize any colors not apparent in nature, to the "normal eye", and curators who had shown a partiality to modern art were replaced by Party members.

CREATION OF THE REICHSKULTURKAMMER

In September 1933 the *Reichskulturkammer* (Reich Culture Chamber) was established, with Joseph Goebbels, Hitler's *Reichminister für Volksaufklärung und Propaganda* (Reich Minister for Public Enlightenment and Propaganda) in charge. Subchambers within the Culture Chamber, representing the individual arts (music, film, literature, architecture, and the visual arts) were created; these were membership groups consisting of "racially pure" artists supportive of the Party, or willing to be compliant. Goebbels made it clear: "In future only those who are members of a chamber are allowed to be productive in our cultural life. Membership is open only to those who fulfil the entrance condition. In this way all unwanted and damaging elements have been excluded." By 1935 the Reich Culture Chamber had 100,000 members. Nonetheless there was, during the period 1933-1934, some confusion within the Party on the question of Expressionism. Goebbels and some others believed that the forceful works of such artists as Emil Nolde, Ernst Barlach and Erich Heckel exemplified the Nordic spirit; as Goebbels explained, "We National Socialists are not unmodern; we are the carrier of a new modernity, not only in politics and in social matters, but also in art and intellectual matters." However, a faction led by Rosenberg despised Expressionism, leading to a bitter ideological dispute which was settled only in September 1934, when Hitler declared that there would be no place for modernist experimentation in the Reich.

Modern artworks were purged from German museums. Over 5,000 works were initially seized, including 1,052 by Nolde, 759 by Heckel, 639 by Ernst Ludwig Kirchner and 508 by Max Beckmann, as well as smaller numbers of works by such artists as Alexander Archipenko, Marc Chagall, James Ensor, Henri Matisse, Pablo Picasso and Vincent van Gogh. These became the material for a defamatory exhibit, *Entartete Kunst* ("Degenerate Art"), featuring over 650 paintings, sculptures, prints, and books from the collections of thirty two German museums, that premiered in Munich on July 19, 1937 and remained on view until November 30 before travelling to eleven other cities in Germany and Austria. In this exhibition, the artworks were deliberately presented in a disorderly manner, and accompanied by mocking labels.

Coinciding with the *Entartete Kunst* exhibition, the *Große Deutsche Kunstausstellung* (Great German art exhibition) made its premiere amid much pageantry. This exhibition, held at the palatial *Haus der deutschen Kunst* (House of German Art), displayed the work of officially approved artists such as Arno Breker and Adolf Wissel. At the end of four months *Entartete Kunst* had attracted over two million visitors, nearly three and a half times the number that visited the nearby *Große Deutsche Kunstausstellung*.

GENRES IN THE THIRD REICH

PAINTING

In general, painting – once purged of "degenerate art" – was based on traditional genre painting. Titles were heavily significant, such as *"Fruitful Land"*, *"Liberated Land"*, *"Standing Guard"*, *"Through Wind and Weather"*, or *"Blessing of Earth."*

Landscape painting featured mostly heavily in the Greater German Art exhibition. While drawing on German Romanticism traditions, it was to be firmly based on real landscape, Germans' *Lebensraum*, without religious moods. Peasants were also popular images, reflecting a simple life in harmony with nature. This art showed no sign of the mechanization of farm work. The farmer

The SS are depicted as the defenders of Germany fighting against the advances of English Jewry.

laboured by hand, with effort and struggle. Not a single painting in the first exhibition showed urban or industrialized life; the exhibition in 1938 contained only two.

Nazi theory explicitly rejected "materialism", and therefore, despite the realistic treatment of images, "realism" was a seldom used term. A painter was to create an ideal picture, for eternity. The images of men, and still more of women, were heavily stereotyped, with physical perfection required for the nude paintings. This may have been the cause of there being very few anti-Semitic paintings; while such works as *Um Haus and Hof*, depicting a Jewish speculator dispossessing an elderly peasant couple exist, they are few, perhaps because the art was supposed to be on a higher plane. Explicitly political paintings were more common but still very rare. Heroic imagery, on the other hand, was common enough to be commented on by a critic: "The heroic element stands out. The worker, the farmer, the soldier are the themes… Heroic subjects dominate over sentimental ones".

With the advent of war, war paintings became far more common. The images were heavily romanticized, depicting heroic sacrifice and victory. Still, landscapes still predominated, and among the painters exempted from war service, all were noted for landscapes or other pacific subjects.

Even Hitler and Goebbels found the new paintings disappointing, although Goebbels tried to put a good face on it with the observation that they had cleared the field, and that these desperate times drew many talents into political life rather than cultural.

SCULPTURE

Sculpture's monumental possibilities gave it a better expression of Nazi racial theories. The Greater German Art Exhibit displayed, throughout Nazi years, a steady rise in the number of sculptures at the expense of paintings. The most common image was of the nude male, expressing the ideal of the Aryan race. Arno Breker's skill at this type made him Hitler's favourite sculptor. Nude females were also common, though they tended to be less monumental. In both cases, the physical form was to show no imperfections.

Josef Thorak was another official sculptor of the Third Reich owing to his skill at monumental sculpture.

MUSIC

Germany's urban centres in the 1920s and 30s were buzzing with jazz clubs, cabaret houses and avant garde music. In contrast, the National Socialist regime made concentrated efforts to shun modern music (which was considered degenerate and Jewish in nature) and instead embraced classical "German" music. Highly favoured was music which alluded to a mythic, heroic German past such as Johann Sebastian Bach, Ludwig van Beethoven and Richard Wagner. The music of Arnold Schoenberg (and atonal music along with it), Gustav Mahler, Felix Mendelssohn and

Die Partei, Arno Breker's statue representing the spirit of the Nazi Party.

many others was banned because they were Jewish or of Jewish origin. Paul Hindemith fled rather than fit his music into Nazi ideology. Some operas of Georg Friederich Händel were either banned outright for themes sympathetic to Jews and Judaism or had new librettos written for them.

Music by non-German composers was tolerated if it classically-inspired, tonal, and not by a composer of Jewish origin or having ties to ideologies hostile to the Third Reich. The Nazis recognized Franz Liszt for having German origin and fabricated a genealogy that purported that Frédéric Chopin was German, and the Nazi Governor-General of occupied Poland even had a "Chopin Museum" built in Warsaw. Music of the Russian Peter Tchaikovsky could be performed in Nazi Germany even after Operation Barbarossa. Operas by Gioacchino Rossini, Giuseppe Verdi and Giacomo Puccini got frequent play. Such contemporary composers as the Russian Igor Stravinsky and Béla Bartók were tolerated until they ran afoul of Nazi politics.

There has been controversy over the use of certain composers' music by the Nazi regime, and whether that implicates the composer as implicitly Nazi. Composers such as Richard Strauss, who served as the first director of the Propaganda Ministry's music division, and Carl Orff have been subject to extreme criticism and heated defence.

Jews were quickly prohibited from performing or conducting classical music in Germany. Such conductors as Otto Klemperer, Bruno Walter, Josef Krips, and Kurt Sanderling fled Germany. Upon the Nazi seizure of Czechoslovakia, the conductor Karel Ančerl was blacklisted as a Jew and was sent in turn to Theresienstadt and Auschwitz.

GRAPHIC DESIGN

The poster became an important medium for propaganda during this period. Combining text and bold graphics, posters were extensively deployed both in Germany and in the areas occupied. Their typography reflected the Nazis' official ideology. The use of Fraktur was common in Germany until 1941, when Martin Bormann denounced the typeface as "*Judenlettern*" and decreed that only Roman type should be used. Modern sans-serif typefaces were condemned as cultural Bolshevism, although Futura continued to be used owing to its practicality.

Imagery frequently drew on heroic realism. Nazi youth and the SS were depicted monumentally, with lighting posed to produce grandeur.

POPULAR ART

Mass culture was less stringently regulated than high culture, possibly because the authorities feared the consequences of too heavy-handed interference in popular entertainment. Thus, until the outbreak of the war, most Hollywood films could be screened, including It Happened One Night, San Francisco, and Gone with the Wind. While performance of atonal music was banned, the prohibition of jazz was less strictly enforced. Benny Goodman and Django Reinhardt were popular, and leading English and American jazz bands continued to perform in major cities until the war; thereafter, dance bands officially played "swing" rather than the banned jazz.

ART THEFT

Later, as the occupiers of Europe, the Germans trawled the museums and private collections of Europe for suitably "Aryan" art to be acquired to fill a bombastic new gallery in Hitler's home town of Linz. At first a pretence was made of exchanges of works (sometimes with Impressionist masterpieces, considered degenerate by the Nazis), but later acquisitions came through forced "donations" and eventually by simple looting.

INDIVIDUAL ARTISTS

In September 1944 the Ministry of Public Enlightenment and Propaganda prepared a list of 1,041 artists considered crucial to National Socialist culture, and therefore exempt from war service. This *Gottbegnadeten* list provides a well-documented index to the painters, sculptors, architects and filmmakers who were regarded by the Nazis as politically sympathetic, culturally valuable, and still residing in Germany at this late stage of the war.

CHAPTER 8

PAYING THE PRICE
GOEBBELS AND STREICHER

ON 1 May, Vice-Admiral Hans-Erich Voss saw Goebbels for the last time: "Before the breakout (from the bunker) began, about ten generals and officers, including myself, went down individually to Goebbels's shelter to say goodbye. While saying goodbye I asked Goebbels to join us. But he replied: 'The captain must not leave his sinking ship. I have thought about it all and decided to stay here. I have nowhere to go because with little children I will not be able to make it'."

The Goebbels family. In this vintage manipulated image, Goebbels' stepson Harald Quandt (who was absent due to military duty) was added to the group portrait.

At 8 pm on the evening of 1 May, Goebbels arranged for an SS dentist, Helmut Kunz, to kill his six children by injecting them with morphine and then, when they were unconscious, crushing an ampule of cyanide in each of their mouths. According to Kunz's testimony, he gave the children morphine injections but it was Magda Goebbels and Stumpfegger, Hitler's personal doctor, who then administered the cyanide. Shortly afterward, Goebbels and his wife went up to the garden of the Chancellery, where they killed themselves. The details of their suicides are uncertain. After the war, Rear-Admiral Michael Musmanno, a U.S. naval officer and judge, published an account apparently based on eye-witness testimony: "At about 8:15 pm, Goebbels arose from the table, put on his hat, coat and gloves and, taking his wife's arm, went upstairs to the garden." They were followed by Goebbels's adjutant, *SS-Hauptsturmführer* Günther Schwägermann. "While Schwägermann was preparing the petrol, he heard a shot. Goebbels had shot himself and his wife took poison. Schwägermann ordered one of the soldiers to shoot Goebbels again because he was unable to do it himself." One SS officer later said they each took cyanide and were shot by an SS trooper. According to another account, Goebbels shot his wife and then himself. This version is portrayed in the movie Downfall.

The bodies of Goebbels and his wife were then burned in a shell crater, but owing to the lack of petrol the burning was only partly effective, and their bodies were easily identifiable. A few days later, Voss was brought back to the bunker by the Soviets to identify the partly burned bodies of Joseph and Magda Goebbels and the bodies of their children. "Vice-Admiral Voss, being asked how he identified the people as Goebbels, his wife and children, explained that he recognized the burnt body of the man as former *Reichsminister* Goebbels by the following signs: the shape of the head, the line of the mouth, the metal brace that Goebbels had on his right leg, his gold NSDAP badge and the burnt remains of his party uniform." The remains of the Goebbels family were repeatedly buried and exhumed, along with the remains of Hitler, Eva Braun, General Hans Krebs and Hitler's dogs. The last burial had been at the SMERSH facility in Magdeburg on 21 February 1946. In 1970, KGB director Yuri Andropov authorised an operation to destroy the remains. On 4 April 1970, a Soviet KGB team with detailed burial charts secretly exhumed five wooden boxes. The remains from the boxes were thoroughly burned and crushed, after which the ashes were thrown into the Biederitz river, a tributary of the nearby Elbe.

Joachim Fest writes: "What he seemed to fear more than anything else was a death devoid of dramatic effects. To the end he was what he had always been: the propagandist for himself. Whatever he thought or did was always based on this one agonizing wish for self-exaltation, and this same object was served by the murder of his children... They were the last victims of an egomania extending beyond the grave. However, this deed, too, failed to make him the figure of tragic destiny he had hoped to become; it merely gave his end a touch of repulsive irony."

JULIUS STREICHER'S FALL FROM POWER, TRIAL AND EXECUTION

When Germany surrendered to the Allied armies in May 1945, Streicher said later, he decided to commit suicide. Instead, he married his former secretary, Adele Tappe. Days later, on 23 May 1945, Streicher was captured in the town of Waidring, Austria, by a group of American officers led by Major Henry Plitt – who

Julius Streicher in custody.

was Jewish. At first Streicher claimed to be a painter named "Joseph Sailer," but after a few questions, quickly admitted to his true identity.

During his trial, Streicher claimed that he had been mistreated by Allied soldiers after his capture. By his account they ordered him to take off his clothes in his cell, burned him with cigarettes and made to extinguish them with his bare feet, allowed him to drink only water from a toilet, made him kiss the feet of Negro soldiers and beat him with a bullwhip. He further claimed that some of the soldiers also spat at him and forced his mouth open to spit in it.

Julius Streicher was not a member of the military and did not take part in planning the Holocaust, or the invasion of other nations. Yet his pivotal role in inciting the extermination of Jews was significant enough, in the prosecutors' judgment, to include him in the indictment of Major War Criminals before the International Military Tribunal – which sat in Nuremberg, where Streicher had once been an unchallenged authority. In essence, the prosecutors took the line that Streicher's incendiary speeches and articles made him an accessory to murder, and therefore as culpable as those who actually ordered the mass extermination of Jews (such as Hans Frank and Ernst Kaltenbrunner).

During his trial, Streicher displayed for the last time the flair for courtroom theatrics that had made him famous in the 1920s. He answered questions from his own defence attorney with diatribes against Jews, the Allies, and the court itself, and was frequently silenced by the court officers. Streicher was largely shunned by all of the other Nuremberg defendants. He also peppered his testimony with references to passages of Jewish texts he had so often carefully selected and inserted (invariably out of context) into the pages of *Der Stürmer*.

Streicher was found guilty of crimes against humanity at the Nuremberg War Crimes Trial and sentenced to death on 1 October 1946. The judgment against him read, in part:

"...For his 25 years of speaking, writing and preaching hatred of the Jews, Streicher was widely known as 'Jew-Baiter Number One.' In his speeches and articles, week after week, month after month, he infected the German mind with the virus of anti-Semitism, and incited the German people to active persecution... Streicher's incitement to murder and extermination at the time when Jews in the East were being killed under the most horrible conditions clearly constitutes persecution on political and racial grounds in connection with war crimes, as defined by the Charter, and constitutes a crime against humanity."

Streicher was hanged in the early hours of 16 October 1946, along with the nine other condemned defendants from the first Nuremberg trial (Göring, Streicher's nemesis, committed suicide only hours earlier). Streicher's was the most melodramatic of the hangings carried out that night. At the bottom of the scaffold he cried out *"Heil Hitler!"*. When he mounted the platform, he delivered his last sneering reference to Jewish scripture, snapping

(Left) A health and safety poster warning against the dangers of fire on farmsteads. (Right) The direct link between the workers and the soldiery at the front is emphasised in this war-time poster.

"Purim-Fest 1946!". The Jewish holiday Purim celebrates the escape by the Jews from extermination at the hands of Haman, an ancient Persian government official. At the end of the Purim story, Haman is hanged, as are his ten sons. Streicher's final declaration before the hood went over his head was, "The Bolsheviks will hang you one day!" Howard K. Smith, who covered the executions, said in his filed report that after the hood descended over Streicher's head, he also said what apparently was *"Adele, meine liebe Frau!"* ("Adele, my dear wife!").

The consensus among eyewitnesses was that Streicher's hanging did not proceed as planned, and that he did not receive the quick death from spinal severing typical of the other executions at Nuremberg. Howard K. Smith, who covered the executions for the International News Service, reported that Streicher "went down kicking" which may have dislodged the hangman's knot from its ideal position. Smith stated that Streicher could be heard groaning under the scaffold after he dropped through the trap-door, and that the executioner intervened under the gallows, which was screened by wood panels and a black curtain, to finish the job. U. S. Army Master Sergeant John C. Woods was the main executioner, and not only insisted he had performed all executions correctly, but stated he was very proud of his work.

APPENDIX

The source: G. Stark, *Moderne politische Propaganda*
(Munich: Verlag Frz. Eher Nachf., 1930).

THE ORGANIZATION OF PROPAGANDA

THE ACKNOWLEDGMENT that only a unified propaganda apparatus has the likelihood of success led the party headquarters and several regional offices (*Gauleitungen*) to create central propaganda offices. Where that has not yet happened, immediate steps should be taken.

The task of these propaganda centrals is to study advertising methods and see how we can use them, which requires above all a well-organized propaganda organization.

To this end each local group must train propaganda wardens, who will lead the entire local propaganda effort and are responsible for its flawless execution in their areas. These propaganda wardens, subordinate to the local and section offices, work closely with the cell leaders and cell officers, as well as with the S.A. It is often a good idea for the propaganda warden to train others in his section or local group to help him with his duties.

Of course, each party member should help out with propaganda. To be a member is to be obligated to serve. The S.A. is also obliged to be ready to serve at any time, regardless of the weather.

Regular party members should be grouped in units to carry out house-to-house propaganda.

A special group, skilled in hanging posters, should not be lacking.

The *Gau* offices provide sections and local groups with guidelines for propaganda. These guidelines should be on paper, and are finding for all sections and local groups. In propaganda department meetings, questions and advice for propaganda wardens will be discussed. Regular meetings of the propaganda wardens discuss current questions of propaganda. Special educational courses provide propaganda wardens with the proper skills. To support what they hear, special notebooks are produced.

The entire collection of propaganda material should generally be produced by the Reich or the *Gau* propaganda offices. Economics of scale save considerable sums.

Although the sections and local groups generally enjoy considerable flexibility, at particular times (e.g., during major campaigns, elections, etc.) they must follow precisely the plans of the propaganda central.

The press office is a branch of the propaganda department. It should receive clippings of all reports of attacks, meeting disturbances, marches and so on from both our own and the enemy press.

THE METHODS OF PROPAGANDA

To carry out propaganda effectively in the cities, it is necessary to understand the proper use of the most important methods of propaganda. It is above all essential that the propaganda warden does not follow advice coming from a desktop, but rather that he is and remains in close contact with the people. Only he who understands everyday life, and who is familiar with events in political life, will be able to speak effectively to the people he wishes to persuade. Without that contact, advertising speaks in a dead language. To see with the eyes of the masses - that is the whole secret of effective propaganda.

There are four kinds of propaganda:
1. Propaganda through the written word,
2. Propaganda through the spoken word,
3. Propaganda through mass marches,
4. Propaganda through cultural gatherings.
1. Propaganda through the written word: flyers, leaflets,

party newspapers and books, advertising circulars, apartment newspapers and factory papers, posters, stamps, other newspapers, N.S. stamps and postcards, banners and billboards, slides, and films. Remember that it is against the law to use walls, building facades, street surfaces, and so on. The following observations apply only to permitted forms of propaganda.

a) Not much needs to be said about the effectiveness of stickers. Their task is to be a constant reminder to the indifferent and to gradually unsettle them. Stickers in the wrong places are usually placed by the enemy to discredit us.

Identical stickers next to each other make a good effect. "Many drops wear away stone" applies here. Incessantly, repeatedly, people must see our stickers!

How should they look? They should be small enough so the person applying them will have enough saliva. They should be brief (few, but vivid words). The layout should be good, with no white space at the edges where graffiti can be written. Each party

(Left) The joy of labour is emphasised in this poster recruiting volunteers for the Labour Battalions. (Right) A war-time drive to convince the populace to deliver much needed items in order to help the war effort.

member should carry such stickers with him. One can apply them quickly and inconspicuously.

b) The flyer, with a few sentences, which is distributed on the street, has lost its effectiveness. It is soon thrown away, and its content, mostly only an announcement of a meeting, is hardly noticed.

Successful small leaflets (30 x 60 mm) that carry texts like this: "National Socialists buy only in German shops. The middle class paper: the *Völkischer Beobachter*."

These small leaflets can be left in shops.

Another promising innovation is flyers with caricatures. A timely sketch by our Mjölnir (a Nazi cartoonist) with an appropriate caption is effective. Good pictures are also effective (e.g., illustrations from the *Angriff* or from the pamphlet *"Those Damned Nazis"*).

Flyers in various colours, but with identical slogans, some with caricatures, spread through entire city districts are effective. For example:

- Against Marxism and Reaction - the National Socialists!
- For Freedom and Bread - the National Socialists!
- Your greeting: *Heil Hitler!*
- Down with the party corpses! Power to the National Socialists!
- Become a National Socialist, all else is shit. The NSDAP has the welfare of the city in mind.

The slogans can be ordered from the propaganda department.

All flyers, leaflets, posters and so on that are posted should be attached in a way that makes them difficult to remove. Random application requires care, and is besides illegal. Our opponents use plate glass successfully; also display windows of German shops.

c) The leaflet should contain a brief, easily understandable idea. It should appeal to the enemy, which demands a certain skill on the part of the writer. The text can be cruder in working class districts, more subtle in the style of the Berlin democratic papers in middle class neighbourhoods. The most important phrases should be in bold or larger type. Tiny text, bad organization and boring material kill interest. The interest of the indifferent, from whom one cannot expect much effort, must be awakened.

The legal issue here is important. The distributor of a leaflet is at risk when information about the printer or author is missing.

Information about distribution is given in rubrics d) and e).

d) Special issues of party newspapers have a special note in red at the top announcing a particular meeting. A rubber stamp can be used for this. Circle the date in red.

A trial subscription to our newspapers can have a remarkable effect on the average person who receives little mail. Don't underestimate the impact of mailing advertising material and meeting invitations to those in the S-Files (Sympathizers file) maintained by local groups and sections. Mail is much more personal. Over time, it has its effects.

Each party member must ask for our newspapers in all restaurants, railway stations, newspaper kiosks and so on.

More than ever, it is important to provide reading rooms with copies of our papers.

And don't forget the little things, to which we owe much success. One always brings newspapers (new and used), leaflets, etc. along. At appropriate times, one "accidentally" leaves them in the train, streetcar, in restaurants, businesses in which one shops, in doctor and dentist offices, at the barber, etc.

Books are such an obvious means of advertising that nothing more needs to be said.

e) The brochures, which in contrast to leaflets provide the reader with more detailed treatments of various issues, suffer the disadvantage of costing sections and local groups considerable money. The Propaganda Department tries to provide these at reasonable prices by printing large numbers. We are preparing a brief version of our party program in an edition of 150,000, which will cost 2 pfennig.

Brochures treating current issues will follow.

Party members in normal clothing are very effective when they distribute such brochures at busy corners. This propaganda is even stronger when the distributor has a sign that says something like "Free Brochure: How Long Will It Go On?" He who understands the psychology of the masses knows that people will take such brochures only when they are free.

Leaflets, free newspapers and brochures should be distributed only in such places where it is likely that they will be read immediately. Good places are in train stations, for those going to a train, not coming from one. People will read on the train, but not on the street. Another example: distribute in the morning at factory gates (not at the end of the shift). Then the material can be read and discussed during the breakfast break. Our leaflets and newspapers are also good reading for those waiting in the unemployment offices, for travellers in long distance trains, etc., anywhere where time must be killed and people will read anything.

The best success comes through the systematic distribution of advertising material from door-to-door. This should be done only on Sunday mornings so that people can read them at their leisure with their morning coffee.

Get every citizen a brochure on Sunday morning!

f) An important method of propaganda is the so-called "neighbourhood newspaper," which, following the Communist example, are produced for a specific area.

They contain news about our neighbourhood activities and about the questions of the day. To keep the sections and local groups free from difficulty with the law, the political part is printed by a central office in the *Gau*. The sections and local groups need to produce only the general section, list the section meetings, the *Gau* meetings, and so on. An effective masthead is important.

g) The factory newspaper is modelled after the neighbourhood newspapers. They are designed only for a single factory and cover work issues and political issues. To make them more interesting, events in the relevant factory are covered. These newspapers are monitored by a central *Gau* office. Typical mastheads: *NSB-Scheinwerfer*, *Siemens-Lautsprecher*, *Lorenz-Aktie*, etc.

h) Posters, despite their considerable cost, are the best form of propaganda, and in relation to their cost a cheap method of advertising.

Posters with text give a brief summary of a meeting and acquaint the reader with the goals of the speaker. It is well known that our textual posters have their own style, such that the attentive observer recognizes from a distance that it is something from the Nazis. Large posters in red must be designed so that they stand out on the poster pillar. A small poster is ineffective, and not in keeping with the significance of our movement. No one reads a poster stuffed with text. The top must be clear enough to draw attention. The bottom must also catch attention. The swastika should be used sparingly at first, particularly in middle class districts.

(Left) A poster designed to assure the populace that Germany's allied enemies will be crushed by the might of a united Germany. (Right) A typical Aryan is depicted in this poster assuring it's audience of certain victory.

The headline must be large; it should dominate the poster. In general, only the name of the party should be emphasized in the text. The text should, as already mentioned, be short and make the meeting topic clear. A mention of our press is also appropriate.

Effective posters emphasize words that create a certain mood and can be noticed from a distance.

A good example was the familiar large poster of *Gau Greater Berlin: Heil Kaiser Dir!*, that had great success because it appeared at the right time (27th January) and at the right places in the proper size.

We are preparing examples of good posters and an article titled "Posters and leaflets from idea to reality."

The text poster fulfils its purpose when, besides the already-mentioned clear content, there is sufficient time to read it. If not, the picture poster is better. The effect of the picture poster lies with its capacity to be understood at a glance, to get across the spiritual attitude instantly, whereas the text poster needs a certain time to read and a longer time to think about. The hurried city-dweller does not have much time. Mostly, he only catches a quick look at a poster while walking past. The picture has to instantly say at a glance everything that a longer text poster says. Herein lies the difficulty. It is hard to find a riveting picture with a few catchy words. There aren't many Mjölnirs (a leading Nazi artist). For us, the picture poster is simply a question of money. Here too we are limited by financial weakness.

The posters from *Gau Berlin* for the Reichstag election of 1928 and the city elections of 1929 are familiar. The Rathenau poster from the "*Angriff,*" halfway between a text and picture poster, had great effect. Unfortunately, it could be used only in a limited way. The illustration will be passed along to the individual *Gau* offices for use in other posters.

The advertising campaign for the "*Angriff*" was imitated by the Ullstein paper "Tempo," though to a degree corresponding to the financial strength of the firm. Our posters were:

Nr. 1. The Attack

Nr. 2. When will the Attack happen?

Nr. 3. "The Attack," the German evening newspaper.

Ullstein did it this way:

1. You lack Tempo!

2. You will soon have Tempo.

3. Tomorrow you will have Tempo.

4. "Tempo", the daily evening newspaper.

The legal side has already been covered in section c) (leaflets).

i) Stamps can be effective when used on letters, newspapers, etc. They should use very short slogans. It's a good idea to carry a stamp with one, in order to be able to use it whenever possible. As already mentioned, other posters may not be stamped; such stamps will be produced by the propaganda offices and distributed to subordinate units.

k) Too little attention is given to the local press, particularly in smaller towns. People learn about the NSDAP only from the standpoint of their party press. Our successes are either ignored or played down. Nonetheless, some local papers with wide readership do not oppose us. These papers are usually willing to print material we provide.

Meeting announcements in the Community Calendar are generally carried. There may be a small charge for longer notices.

Always send newspapers a brief, objective, but nonetheless informative meeting report for their local sections.

Advertisements in the middle class press are usually very expensive and only support the enemy. They should be used only when absolutely necessary. Favourable treatment of the meeting should be made a condition of buying an advertisement.

l) Stamps, which the Reich Propaganda Office produces in an attractive manner, are not lacking in effect. They can be placed on the first page of letters, on cards and so on in the bottom third. The price varies from 1/2 to 2 pfennig. The price of these stamps finances other propaganda.

Postcards of the movement should be sent to friends and acquaintances at every opportunity. They may even have an impact on republican letter carriers.

m) A simple but still effective form of propaganda is the banners with short slogans that hang in our large meetings. They can be used in smaller versions on trucks and vans. In such cases, be sure to protect them. Bicycle columns too can be used for propaganda.

n) Another method is the so-called railway track advertising. With the permission of the property owner, signs can be erected. The *"Völkischer Beobachter"* has won a large number of new subscriptions in this way.

Rooftop advertising is also useful, Unfortunately, it is expensive when the approval of the owner is required.

o) The use of slide shows and film depends on the available means. The party's first films have already been produced by the central office and *Gau Berlin*. A major film is in the works. We too should use the most modern advertising methods to serve our movement.

2. Propaganda through the spoken word: Propaganda by the spoken word - talking with the individual, study groups, discussion evenings, mass meetings, choruses - usually result from the written word. The two forms of propaganda are inseparable.

a) The most basic form of oral propaganda is the discussion with the individual. This form is still the most effective, since deep contact is established. It is easier to do that in this way than in study groups.

b) The study group deepens the idea and educates the party member, and encourages closer contact with citizens who are friendly or at least honestly uncertain about the movement. Through them we win supporters by give and take. Without doubt, the movement from its beginnings built the inner strength it needed and won its best fighters through study groups. Every local group should hold two study groups a month. If in a given month no public meeting is held, it should hold another study group.

A discussion evening is not a membership meeting, open only to a certain audience, but rather a public gathering to which party members may bring guests or truth-seeking racial comrades.

Securing a speaker is not as great a problem as in a public people's meeting, Party members not rhetorically suited for a larger public meeting can do very well in a discussion evening, as long as they possess a firm grasp of the aims of the movement.

They will become increasingly better speakers, and the give-and-take with party members will help them become able to serve as discussion speakers at the meetings of other parties.

The speaker is the propagandist of the idea, who sacrifices his time, strength, health and welfare for the movement. Recognizing his ability and caring for him provides support he needs.

It is a matter of honour for a speaker to meet his obligations insofar as it is humanly possible. Meetings should be held regardless of the attendance. The credibility of the party is at stake.

(Left) Germany is characterised as the protector of Europe against the Bolshevists and Jews. (Right) Victory or Bolshevism, as the clouds of war darkened the stark choice was becoming clear. There is nothing optimistic about this poster from 1943.

The speaker should keep in mind that although his activity in study evenings promises little fame, they often bring more success for the movement than a public meeting.

e) The public mass meeting is the place where an authoritative speaker proclaims the aims of our movement and the nature of our world view with regard to domestic and international events to every class of the population. The meeting is therefore a matter of the prestige of the party and a source of strength. The manner of its preparation is the mark of a good local group or section. One should speak of a "mass meeting" only when the masses will really appear.

The theme of the meeting should always be chosen to reach the people, particularly the group that one wants to attract to the meeting. We distinguish between world view and current event themes.

The other way to chose meeting themes is to find sensational events, scandals of the Jews or Marxists, in particular events that can be summarized in three or four words. This encourages the masses to come from curiosity, anger over political events, or in the hope of hearing something advantageous given their financial or class interests.

Do not neglect either world view or political themes. Otherwise, one either loses contact with the masses, or on the other hand attracts only the masses, not the valuable fighters we need. The goal is to build the enthusiasm of the masses from meeting to meeting so that they are eager to come, as was achieved in an exemplary manner in Munich during the years 1922/23.

The following principles for conducting meetings apply:
1. Before the meeting, the speaker should be informed of the local political situation.
2. The meeting chair, with a witness, should assume control from the host.
3. Meeting protection should be assured either by a sufficient number of local or neighbouring S.A. men, or by request

to the police. The latter is particularly important in the case of meetings that may turn violent, for the riot damage act requires it. The state's responsibilities begin only when damages exceed 400 marks.

4. It has proven advantageous in certain meetings and in certain places to have a part of the S.A. in civilian dress scattered throughout the room in order to deal with expected troublemakers.

5. The chairman conducts the meeting. His introduction and conclusion should be at most 3-5 minutes.

6. Attendance by party members is both expected and tactically necessary, given the opponents. No party member should want to demonstrate, either by not appearing at all or by being inattentive, that he already knows everything that the speaker has to say.

7. In the discussion period, only one speaker from each party is permitted. Announce at the start that a speaker cannot give his speaking time to someone else. It is better in advance to give a speaker from another party a longer speaking time, if that is required by the local situation.

8. At the start of each discussion speech at difficult meetings, it is good to announce the time to the audience to keep the discussion speaker and his supporters from claiming that he has only spoken for 5 or 10 minutes.

9. Make propaganda during the meeting for the central organ of the movement, the "*Völkischer Beobachter*," either through brief words from the chairman or before the meeting and during the breaks with brochures.

10. Each meeting is to be closed by the chairman with a "*Heil*" to National Socialism and our Führer Adolf Hitler.

11. Singing a song at the conclusion of a meeting makes sense only if this can be done well. The meeting chairman should give directions. It is to be sung standing up, not by singing one stanza as people are leaving. Thin and

scattered voices by several party members make a bad impression, particularly when the opponent begins to sing his battle song.

If many communists are present, do not close with the national anthem. The following case demonstrates this. One of our well-known speakers spoke to a meeting with a predominately communist audience. After he had impressively demonstrated the whole miserable swindle of Bolshevist equality to the audience, the chairman wanted to close the successful meeting with the national anthem. The speaker whispered to him "don't sing the national anthem!" The chairman said: "At the request of the speaker, we won't sing the national anthem!" This stupidity led the communists to say that we had good speakers, but were still reactionaries, while the *Stahlhelm* members present thought we were concealed Marxists after all!

(Left) A poster proclaiming the might of the anti-aircraft defences as Germany's shield against allied bombers. In fact, there was little propaganda could hope to achieve when faced with the reality. (Right) A volksturm recruiting poster from 1944.

d) Choruses supported by a trumpet are effective. Several short, compelling sentences, repeated often, have a strong effect on a meeting. Be sure they have practiced, and are not in an awkward position.

3. Propaganda through mass marches: The third type of propaganda includes Demonstrations, local S.A. marches, *Gau* and Reich party rallies. Here all that needs to be said is that good discipline is the best propaganda.

4. Propaganda through cultural gatherings: Cultural gatherings are the fourth group. The influence of theatre and movies on the masses is well known. One has to think only of Piscator or of Russian films like *"Battleship Potemkin"* and *"The General Line."* We must try to use these institutions for our purposes, and to combat the destructive influence of cultural Bolshevism. The *N.S. Volksbühne* and the *N.S. Filmbühne* have been established in some cities already and have done well. They are not only a recreational outlet for party members, but also promotional gatherings. Our theatre presents only works displaying the German spirit. *The N.S. Filmbühne*, which strives to produce our own films, also shows films that put heroic thoughts in the foreground.

In order to use our films every day, we should attempt to supplement political speeches with films in the suburbs. Even the smallest cell can be reached and informed in this way.

This has been only a survey of propaganda. It must be used in various ways, but will be successful only when it is conducted by fanatical fighters with unbreakable wills.

MORE FROM THE SAME SERIES

Most books from 'The Third Reich from Original Sources' series are edited and endorsed by Emmy Award winning film maker and military historian Bob Carruthers, producer of Discovery Channel's Line of Fire and Weapons of War and BBC's Both Sides of the Line. Long experience and strong editorial control gives the military history enthusiast the ability to buy with confidence.

The series advisor is David McWhinnie, producer of the acclaimed Battlefield series for Discovery Channel. David and Bob have co-produced books and films with a wide variety of the UK's leading historians including Professor John Erickson and Dr David Chandler.

Where possible the books draw on rare primary sources to give the military enthusiast new insights into a fascinating subject.

For more information visit www.pen-and-sword.co.uk